PRAISE FOR *MINDFULNESS FOR CHOCOLATE LOVERS*

"*Mindfulness for Chocolate Lovers* provides scientifically supported, yet simple, practical tools for helping us along the road to happiness. The concepts are clear and help break through the confusion and inaccuracies disseminated by different sources about what happiness is, how it can be achieved, and maintained." —**Russell Crane**, PhD, LMFT, editor of *Contemporary Family Therapy* and emeritus professor, Marriage and Family Therapy, Brigham Young University

"An empowering and hopeful book that offers practical ways we can all slow down, exhale, and linger in joy, gratitude, and inner calm." —**Stephen Mardell**, MFT, clinical director, Child and Family Therapy Center

"*Mindfulness for Chocolate Lovers* is a delicious and simple guide to alleviate stress and anxiety. The exercises are fun, the content makes it possible for readers to learn how to be in the moment with ease and intention, as well as learning to be okay when uncomfortable. It's not just about smelling the roses, it's about eating the chocolate, too! I will be recommending it to all my patients." —**Laura Rhodes–Levin**, LMFT, founder of The Missing Peace-Center for Anxiety

"Readers will find *Mindfulness for Chocolate Lovers* to be a therapeutic book that opens the heart, touches the spirit, and expands the mind. Diane R. Gehart artfully and vulnerably offers her expertise and experience, weaving humor, research, and spiritual teachings to lead readers toward growth and groundedness. A must-read for anyone healing from pain or longing for more." —**Jessica ChenFeng**, PhD, LMFT, associate director of Physician Vitality, Loma Linda University Health

"Gehart deliciously unwraps the depths of life secrets in this profoundly accessible book that teaches us the golden rule of attaining true happiness." —**Gerald Monk**, PhD, author of *Intercultural Counseling: Bridging the Us and Them*

"A refreshingly fun and sweet take on mindfulness and joyful living. Diane's gift for translating ancient Eastern philosophies into everyday contexts shines in this approachable yet in-depth contemporary guide." —**Bettina Bush**, editor-at-large, *Working Mother* magazine, and host of Working Mother Radio

"*Mindfulness for Chocolate Lovers* is an intelligent and humorous guide for anyone who is seeking greater happiness and fulfillment. The wisdom, techniques, exercises, and antidotes each give the reader an opportunity for both education and self-discovery." —**Stacy Kaiser**, psychotherapist and author of *How to Be a Grown Up: The Ten Secret Skills Everyone Needs to Know*

Mindfulness for Chocolate Lovers

Mindfulness for Chocolate Lovers

A Lighthearted Way to Stress Less and Savor More Each Day

Diane R. Gehart, PhD

ROWMAN & LITTLEFIELD
Lanham • Boulder • New York • London

Published by Rowman & Littlefield
An imprint of The Rowman & Littlefield Publishing Group, Inc.
4501 Forbes Boulevard, Suite 200, Lanham, Maryland 20706
www.rowman.com

6 Tinworth Street, London SE11 5AL, United Kingdom

Distributed by NATIONAL BOOK NETWORK

British Library Cataloguing in Publication Information Available

Library of Congress Cataloging-in-Publication Data

Names: Gehart, Diane R., 1969– author.
Title: Mindfulness for chocolate lovers : a lighthearted way to stress less and savor more each day / Diane R. Gehart.
Description: Lanham : Rowman & Littlefield, [2019] | Includes bibliographical references and index.
Identifiers: LCCN 2018060861 (print) | LCCN 2019016433 (ebook) | ISBN 9781538129074 (electronic) | ISBN 9781538129067 (pbk. : alk. paper)
Subjects: LCSH: Chocolate industry. | Chocolate. | Comfort food.
Classification: LCC HD9200.A2 (ebook) | LCC HD9200.A2 G44 2019 (print) | DDC 641.3/374—dc23
LC record available at https://lccn.loc.gov/2018060861

∞™ The paper used in this publication meets the minimum requirements of American National Standard for Information Sciences—Permanence of Paper for Printed Library Materials, ANSI/NISO Z39.48-1992.

Dedicated to those who refuse to lose their sense of humor and grace, even during life's darkest moments.

Contents

Author's Introduction: Would You Rather Eat Chocolate than Meditate? ix

Warning: Couch Potatoes and Voyeurs xi

1 Chocolate Meditation: A Taste of the Good Life 1

2 From Chocoholism to Chocolate Snobbery:
Becoming a Seeker of Extraordinary Happiness 11

3 Chocolate Is a Vegetable: Mapping the Truths You
Live By 25

4 Who Moved My Chocolate? Befriending Problems,
Befriending Life 47

5 One Bite Is All It Takes: Mindfully Waking Up
to Your Life 71

6 With or Without Nuts? Crazy Wisdom and the
Back Door to Happiness 97

7 Fierce Compassion: Opening Your Heart to Milk, White,
and Dark 113

8 There's No Wrong Way to Eat a Reese's—Or Is There?
Ethics and Happiness 133

9 Artificial Chocolate and Comfort Foods: Dangers and
Pitfalls on the Path 149

10 The Art of Savoring: Joyfulness as a Way of Life 165

Notes: Academic Bits and Pieces	173
Bibliography	181
Acknowledgments	187
Index	189
About the Author	199

Author's Introduction

Would you rather eat chocolate than meditate? Me too. In this book, you will learn how to do both at the same time while transforming your life using well-established principles for living more fully. The fundamentals to cultivating an unshakable sense of inner joy have been known for centuries—2,600 years to be exact. With stunningly precise parallels, both ancient wisdom and modern science identify the same key elements to joyful living. The problem with getting this message out seems to be poor marketing. Neither the ancients nor scientific researchers have done a great job of making the road attractive or accessible to the average person in the twenty-first century. To further confuse matters, most of what the popular media and common sense teach about happiness is incorrect, sending us in the wrong direction from the start.

After twenty-five years of helping thousands of people lead more fulfilling lives, I found two ingredients that made this knowledge palatable to almost everyone regardless of life situation, education, cultural background, or income level: chocolate and humor. The former entices you to start the journey, and the latter makes it entertaining enough to keep you moving forward. After all, *the pursuit of happiness should be fun.*

As a practitioner, professor, and researcher of psychotherapy, I have carefully studied what leads to happiness and how people change for decades. I have continuously sought to discern what helps people find and sustain the happiness they seek. The answers are surprisingly consistent and clear. In this book, I will share with you my discoveries.

First, I will debunk popular myths that have us looking for happiness in all the wrong places (chapter 2), and then I will construct an accurate map for getting where we want to go (hint: it's not a treasure map; chapter 3). Next, you will learn the hardest but ultimately most liberating lesson: making friends with life and all that is, including the good, the bad, and the ugly—which includes black widow spiders for some of us (chapter 4). From there, you will learn surprisingly playful and palatable options for maximizing your joy, including mindfulness, crazy wisdom, compassion, and ethical living (chapters 5–8). If you have avoided meditation and similar practices for most of your life because they are dull and boring, you may find something that suits your refined and zesty taste for living here. Finally, I teach you how to avoid—or at least survive—the common pitfalls and the dangerous snakes that line the path from where you are to where you want to go (chapter 9). Along the way, I promise numerous opportunities to laugh, to cry, and to reconnect with the best within yourself. You will suddenly discover your most desperate challenges dissolving before you, revealing an easier path and renewing your delight in living and loving. Worst-case scenario: you will have educational excuses to savor some chocolate delights, enjoy a few good laughs, and gain a handful of new insights about your life.

Whether you are reeling from a devastating breakup; feeling adrift professionally; struggling with depression, anxiety, or more severe mental health issues; or simply wanting to feel happier given the numerous blessings in your life, this book will help you make changes that you could never accomplish before because you will now be motivated to *do* something different. I assure you that you won't have to do much: small, tiny steps—with frequent chocolate rewards.

Ultimately, this book invites you to play. To laugh. To love. To heal old heartbreaks. To overcome what was once impossible. To open your heart to life and all it has to offer: white, milk, and dark. The stresses of modern life often create the illusion that life is hard, painful, and lonely. You are only a few bites away from an entirely different approach to living a sweeter life. There is nothing but a wrapper and that nagging inner naysayer stopping you from beginning the journey right now! Although you may find a tempting excuse or two, there is no reason to linger. An easier, more joyful life is effortlessly within reach. Thank you for daring to share the adventure with me.

Your companion on the journey of a lifetime,
Diane R. Gehart, PhD
Westlake Village (LA-ish), California

Warning: Couch Potatoes and Voyeurs

This is not a book for couch potatoes, voyeurs, or those who live life on the sidelines. This is a book for those who want to make a tangible, measurable difference in their lives and in their happiness. That type of change requires getting off the couch and into the real world. Thankfully, chocolate can be found in the real world—so can fun and adventure. So, you will be asked to get out of the comfort zone of your couch and take action: meditate, take a quiz, answer questions, create a map, experiment, and make small changes in your everyday life. I encourage you to push yourself—or perhaps entice yourself with little chocolate rewards—to do as many of these exercises as possible along the way. They may seem silly at first, but I promise you they have been carefully designed to create real change. So, if you are ready for a little adventure, read on!

• 1 •

Chocolate Meditation

A Taste of the Good Life

Before you begin: please grab a piece of wrapped chocolate prior to sitting down to read this chapter, but do not eat it until instructed.

As a psychotherapist working with adults, couples, and families for more than twenty-five years, I have spent more than half my life motivating people to do things they do not want to do. Most who come to me have a good idea of what will improve their situation. For example, virtually all parents believe they have better options than screaming to persuade their children to do homework or complete their chores, but they find themselves yelling anyway. My millennial couples know that turning off their digital devices to have uninterrupted, face-to-face conversations with their partners would likely strengthen their communication and sense of intimacy; nevertheless, there is a blue glow from the bedroom, and American couples are having less sex than ever. Those who seek my help for depression and anxiety are rarely surprised to learn that exercise, healthy eating, sufficient sleep, journaling, and stress reduction techniques like mindfulness are likely to lift their moods. Yet, rates for these disorders are at an all-time high, with 18 percent of adults and 25 percent of children currently having an anxiety disorder and 10 percent of adults and 12 percent of teens experiencing a major depressive episode in the past year. For most, the main struggle is not lack of knowledge about how to solve their problems. Google provides that. What they are missing is *motivation* and the willingness to *follow through* with the actions they know will help their situations.

Grounded in some of the first psychological experiments that involved teaching cats to pump levers for treats, one of the most basic

1

psychological principles is that people can be motivated to change behaviors with positive and negative reinforcement. Although punishment may result in a rapid change in the short term, positive rewards are more likely to result in long-term, sustained change. Thus, as a therapist, I am always seeking ways to entice people to follow through on healthier behaviors by using meaningful rewards.

When I began teaching mindfulness over two decades ago, I discovered that chocolate dramatically increased interest in an otherwise boring activity to most in the Western world. In its most common form, mindfulness involves sitting still in a room by yourself, watching yourself breathe, while trying not to indulge in any thought, itch, noise, or other distraction. For many, this seems an unnecessary form of torture, no matter what the research says about its endless benefits to those in an information-soaked, overstimulated society. But when I added chocolate, interest increased considerably in this dull yet healthy habit.

CHOCOLATE MEDITATION

Rather than rattle off statistics or share success stories, let's begin with a chance for you to have a small taste of mindfulness. During the next five minutes, you have an opportunity to personally experience some essential truths about happiness that go against popular beliefs about what *ought* to make a person happy. Most of us need firsthand experiences like this exercise to convince ourselves to make the commitments required for real change. The insights from Chocolate Meditation No. 1 (yes, there are more to come) will serve as a springboard for addressing attitudes and habits that limit our experience of happiness; we will explore these insights in depth in the chapters ahead.

Chocolate meditation is a variation of the classic mindfulness eating meditation made popular by Jon Kabat-Zinn, who is a pioneer of mindfulness in the West.[1] Most often, mindful eating is done with a raisin, which is also an enlightening exercise. However, I prefer chocolate—both for the taste and for the challenge. Mindfulness is relatively simple with neutral objects, and—for most of us—raisins do not evoke strong emotions. However, many of us have strong opinions, emotions, and even fantasies related to chocolate.

Finally, it's time to make use of that wrapped chocolate sitting next to you. At this moment, you are probably tempted to skip doing this exercise and just read along, but I encourage you to try it. Many books explain why you are where you are in your life and offer advice about how to improve your situation. This book is different because it is intended to create real and measurable change in your daily life. To achieve this change requires *action*: doing something different. So, let's take our first mindful bite!

CHOCOLATE MEDITATION NO. 1

If you prefer a guided meditation, you can find it at www.mindfulnessforchoco latelovers.com. Otherwise, please grab a wrapped chocolate and follow this meditation guide:

Observe It Wrapped

Pick up your wrapped chocolate and imagine you have never seen anything like this object before. You may want to imagine that you are a space alien who has never seen anything like it. Become intensely curious about this object. Then, notice the following:

- *Colors:* Notice the various shades of color and how they may change when the light reflects off the wrapper.
- *Shape and Weight:* Notice its shape and contours. If there is writing on the object, try to view the letters without seeing them as letters—just as shapes. If there is a picture, can you just notice how the colors and shapes come together without labeling the image? Notice the weight, and if it is similar or different in each hand.
- *Scent:* Move it toward your nose and see if you notice a scent.

Unwrap

Now, unwrap it and listen to the sound it makes as you do so.

Observe It Unwrapped

- *Colors:* Again, notice the various shades of color and how they change with the light.
- *Shape and Weight:* Notice the shape and contours of the unwrapped chocolate.

- *Scent:* Move it toward your nose and see if you notice a scent and if it is similar or different from that of the wrapped chocolate.
- *Texture:* Notice the texture. Is it hard, soft, smooth, bumpy? If it is starting to melt, observe that texture and notice your emotional reaction without wiping your fingers.

Observe the Mind

Bring the morsel toward your mouth but *do not* bite into it yet.

- **Body Reaction:** Notice how your body reacts. Do you notice any changes in your mouth? Do you start to salivate? Notice if any other parts of your body are anticipating the bite you are about to take.
- **Mind Reaction:** Now notice the thoughts that are going through your head. Are you excited, frustrated, angry, hesitant? Try to observe thoughts and feelings. You might want to try imagining that you are watching those thoughts and feelings move through your head like clouds across the sky.

Take a Mindful Bite

Take a small bite and let it linger on your tongue. Slowly roll the object around and allow the flavors to move around your mouth.

- *Taste:* What does it taste like? Is the taste different on different parts of your tongue? Is it sweet, salty, bitter, sour, fruity, nutty? I invite you to refrain from judging the taste as good or bad, preferred or unpreferred, or better or worse than a previous experience. Try to simply experience the various taste sensations you are having in the present moment.
- *Feeling:* Take a moment to experience the textures and feeling in your mouth. Perhaps roll the chocolate around some more and see what you notice and if anything changes.
- *Chew:* If you haven't done so already, slowly start chewing and notice how the texture or taste may change as you do so. Continue mindfully eating, slowly taking a bite and experiencing the aroma, texture, flavors. . . . When you are done, just sit quietly for a moment to reflect on your experience of eating this familiar food.

CHOCOLATE-COVERED WISDOM

Having done this exercise with literally thousands of people around the world, I have noticed there are several common reactions and insights that follow. For example, many self-proclaimed chocoholics discover that they like the taste of chocolate less than they thought. Some who say they never cared much for chocolate find that there is more there than they imagined. Inevitably, everyone learns a little something new about themselves and the way they approach their life—or at least chocolate. As we probe a little deeper, this exercise illuminates many simple yet profound truths that offer clues to the happiness we seek.

"IT" IS RIGHT UNDER OUR NOSES

As a professional working mother of two young boys, I sometimes wonder if it was easier to find happiness when humans had fewer "modern conveniences" and spent less time in line, online, and in transit. But, apparently, the ancients struggled with finding happiness as much as those of us in modern times. Laotzu, an ancient Daoist thinker who lived more than three thousand years ago, taught that one does not need to journey to far places or practice special rituals to find joy and peace because it is always here in the *present moment*.[2] Many find that chocolate meditation poignantly underscores the truth in Daoist wisdom: when you slow down to the present moment, a natural sense of ease and peace arises. The enticing excitement and related dramas of the outside world cloud the inherent state of wellness within that emerges when we quiet inner chatter.

This meditation invites us to focus our attention differently than we typically do, and in doing so we find the essence of what we ultimately seek is right here—under our noses. When we focus on what is in the present moment, there is a clear sense of wholeness and that elusive sense of joy that we often seek in the wrong places. For example, many of us assume that true happiness is not possible without certain conditions: in meeting the "one," achieving a meaningful career goal, purchasing a (bigger) home, having a million followers, or buying the latest, coolest gadget. Like most of us, I have spent many years looking everywhere, desperate to find "It." Perhaps a cosmic joke, the frantic search seems necessary for most of us to finally give up, sit down, and realize: *it is right here*. The good news is that inner wellness is much closer than we realize. And you can rightfully laugh and shake your head when you finally stumble upon how simple it is to access.

SLOW DOWN

Practitioners of chocolate meditation report that the exercise highlights how they typically miss the confection's joy by popping it into their mouth without slowing down from their busy pace to actually taste it. We live in a society that frequently equates faster and more with being better. But this simple exercise highlights how misguided these ideas are. Often, someone remarks, "How is it that I have eaten 1,000 pieces of chocolate but when I eat my 1,001st piece mindfully, it is as though I have never actually tasted it before?" Most report that chocolate tastes better eaten more slowly and that they feel less of a need to have a second piece. By making them slow down and experience chocolate through all the senses, the exercise brings significantly more pleasure and happiness than the mindless eating most of us practice daily. For a rare moment, they are fully present to what is happening in their lives and in their bodies, and most cannot help but smile as they enjoy such a sweet moment. The takeaway message is that our experience changes when we change how we focus and what we focus on.

UNEXPECTED BEAUTY

After having done this exercise with a large audience many times, my favorite part is not the taste of chocolate but the sound it makes: the moment when silence is broken by hundreds of people unwrapping their chocolates in unison. The typically unremarkable sound of unwrapping a single chocolate becomes an unexpected symphony when the group works in harmony. It sounds like a waterfall or mountain stream. It is the most delicious moment but also a humbling moment. How many times each day do each of us miss the beauty and pleasures that surround us? When you learn to recognize beauty, it is everywhere: flowers on the side of the road at a stop light; blue sky after the rain; the arch of the old oak tree you pass each day. Similarly, pleasurable experiences surround us also: a cool breeze, the taste of cold water on a hot day, the spray when you bite into a piece of fruit. The happiness we seek is closer than most of us realize; chocolate meditation reminds us that it is a matter of paying attention.

REALITY IS LIKE PLAY-DOH

One of the subtler insights of this meditation comes from the jolt at the end when one returns to everyday reality. This shock reminds us that another reality is always there—you need only shift gears to find it. It is not realistic to think one can or should spend each moment of every day in the bliss of chocolate meditation, but it is realistic to strive to spend more moments of each day in such a state.

If you so choose, at any moment you can shift your reality, reshaping it like a child playing with Play-Doh. The power to shift reality comes from our ability to choose the focus of our attention. For example, in one study, public hospital physicians were divided into three groups: one journaling about things for which they were thankful, the second journaling about their stressors, and the third not journaling at all. Only the physicians maintaining a gratitude journal saw reductions in depressive symptoms and stress.[3] This cleverly designed study highlights that the physicians' improvement came not from the act of journaling itself, but rather from shifting their focus to the positive.

We each make hundreds of small decisions each day about where to focus that can increase or decrease our happiness. For example, when stuck at the slowest line at the store with two impatient kids, I can get frustrated with the wait or instead tune in to the fact that I have some free time to focus on my children and use the time to play a fun game or chat with them. Obviously, if the long wait is making us late for some other obligation, it is tempting to freak out even more—but I have found that does not make the line move faster and serves only to make me miserable and less capable of handling the delay with grace and ease.

SUSPICIOUS OF WHAT YOU WANT

For some, one startling discovery from chocolate meditation is the realization that their thoughts about chocolate do not match the reality. Chocolate holds a mystique for many—the ultimate food of pleasure and indulgence. However, practitioners of chocolate meditation come to see it in a more realistic light, often realizing that it is not the quantity of chocolate that brings pleasure but the quality of one's attention. Some are surprised to discover that they do not like chocolate as much as they tell themselves they do. For others, there is a tinge of disappointment or loss as they realize that their stories about chocolate in their heads are different from the actual experience.

But in another way, it is freeing. One is freed to more consciously make choices related to chocolate as well as other possibilities for feeling similar joys. Once you realize it was not the chocolate that was so special but the *story* or *myth* about the chocolate that made it so, you are beginning to see the mechanics of how we generate happiness. As you learn to mindfully watch the stories in your head about what is "good" and what is "bad" and "what I want" and "what I don't want," there is a strong possibility that you will be able to find happiness in more places than you currently do.

THE PLAN: CHOCOLATE, MINDFULNESS, AND YOU

This book is designed to teach you practical skills that will allow you to more consciously choose how you respond to life's challenges, no matter how big or small. The chapters that follow outline seven steps for increasing happiness developed from positive psychology (the science of happiness), Buddhist psychology, mindfulness, and lessons I have learned (usually the hard way) as a psychotherapist over the past twenty-five years. These seven basic steps include

1. demystifying happiness,
2. identifying common barriers to happiness,
3. befriending reality,
4. shifting your relationship to your mind and life,
5. learning to play with crazy wisdom,
6. developing compassion for self and others, and
7. living an ethical and meaningful life.

Thankfully, modern science and ancient wisdom generally agree on how to best create meaningful happiness in life. The problem is that most of us have habits and beliefs that unintentionally limit our happiness. Even when we struggle to let go of these, we find it hard to do so even with professional help. For example, 50 percent of people who are treated for major depressive disorder—with medication, psychotherapy, or both—will relapse within a year.[4] Strangely, most find that the comfort of the familiar (even if it is dysfunctional) outweighs the potential of a better future, like a child who clings to his favorite teddy bear instead of reaching for a novel toy. My years as a therapist have taught me that most of us need a strong motivator—something enticing and easily doable—to let go of the old ways and embrace the new. In this book, my plan is to use chocolate to lure you away from the unhelpful familiar habits toward a more joyful life.

This may seem too corny to work or take seriously. But, strangely, most find such a playful approach the most effective way to generate happiness rather than serious and rigorous methods, which are incongruent with the final goal. Although a more academic and formal methodology seems as though it would be more appropriate for addressing such an important matter, in my clinical practice, such logical approaches rarely have much effect. Upon reflection, it does make sense that a playful approach might be the best way to increase one's sense of happiness.

From Chocoholism
to Chocolate Snobbery

Becoming a Seeker of Extraordinary Happiness

$\mathcal{A}$s with many others, chocolate has always held a special place in my life. As a child, I didn't make distinctions about quality because I was focused on quantity: how much chocolate will my parents allow me and then how much can I later sneak without them knowing? Over the years, I evolved into a bit of a chocolate snob: I insist on the best and leave the rest. Truthfully, the main motivation for this shift was the less-than-glamorous problem of weight management, which forces me to be more selective with calorie-rich foods. The guiding question became, Is this piece of chocolate worth the extra gym time?

As mindfully savoring each bite became a habit, I became even more of a snob. My first major discernment was that although Americans are the undisputed experts in chocolate-peanut combinations, they sometimes can be waxy. So you have to read the labels, and as I did, I learned there are cultural patterns of note. Belgians have mastered creamy—both the chocolate itself and the fillings. Mexican, Spanish, and South American chocolatiers get the wildest with their recipes, adding chilies, corn, sunflower seeds, rice, and things you least expect to be chocolate-covered. The Brits like theirs extra sweet, and the Swiss have perfected the art of the bar. However, after much searching, I discovered my true love: chocolate hazelnut confections from Italy—the perfect balance of crunchy and smooth. Unfortunately, my children have inherited the same gene, and our family chocolate bills are high, with my boys the only ones in the neighborhood uninterested in freely distributed Halloween treats that do not meet specific chocolate parameters for their young but refined palates.

But the snobbery did not end there. More recently, single-origin chocolates have refined the palate even further. Home to the first cocoa cultivators, Mexico grows beans that are fruity and floral, which is distinct from Ecuador's earthy, tropical flavors, Arriba's notes of rose and hazelnut, and Santo Domingo's scent of tea and berries. Across the ocean in Africa, Cameroon's chocolate hints of butterscotch and almonds and Tanzania's of spice and charcoal. In Asia, Java's cacao is sweet with hints of caramel and toffee, while Papua New Guinea's has deep flavors of cappuccino and smoked wood. I have yet to carefully evaluate the budding cacao from Hawaii grown in rich volcanic soil— the next chocolate-coated frontier. Pondering the possibilities flatlines the brain with delight.

Now each bite connects me to faraway lands and people, appreciating that natural and human labor that each bite represents. I enjoy chocolate as I always have—but for entirely different reasons from when I was a child. This process has helped me discover that there is an art to becoming a *gracious consumer*, not only of chocolate but of life: the joy you receive from an experience has less to do with what or how much you have and more to do with how you relate to it. This is a truth I observed in my first meeting with a master of joyful living.

SAFFRON AND MAROON ROBES

When I was an undergraduate at William and Mary, I had a chance to hear a talk on Buddhism by a resident Tibetan Buddhist monk speaking at the University of Virginia. After a long drive, I arrived at an old home that was converted into a small religious center. The creaky floorboards announced my late entrance as I stepped into the former living room that was now a lecture hall. Wrapped in saffron and maroon robes, the teacher sat quietly at the front of the room, which was filled with eager students of all ages and backgrounds. The setting was simple, but the talk was not. With a heavy accent, he spoke about the finer points of Buddhist philosophy, explaining concepts rarely discussed in the West: dharma, impermanence, non-being, emptiness, bodhisattvas, precepts, and innumerable states of consciousness not listed in any Western psychological text. My head was spinning, trying to understand the philosophical distinctions he was making. At the same time, my heart was encompassed by a deep sense of peace and joy. As the day went on, the peace he radiated drowned out the philosophical ramblings in my head. I no longer remember the points he was trying to make with his words, but I will never forget the lesson he taught with his presence: *True happiness is an inside job.*

His presence provided evidence for a form of happiness I had never seen or heard of before—a joy that was palpable, radiating from his being and seeming to directly enter my own heart. I was deliriously happy for no good reason. It shattered my prior view of happiness as a natural response to things going well in my life. I finally saw how happiness—or more correctly, joy—was an attitude, a choice, a way of life.

SETTLING FOR ORDINARY HAPPINESS

When it comes to seeking happiness, keeping up with the Joneses, the Kardashians, or your ostentatious neighbor is the name of the game for most of us—especially when you look at our actions rather than listen to our words. Few of us would admit to this and, in fact, go to great lengths to pronounce that it is the "little things" that bring true happiness. But when do most of us spontaneously talk of being "happy"? Typically, it is when we are able to purchase the house, car, clothes, vacation, and gadgets of our dreams—or at least what our friends, family, and the media define as our dreams. We say we are happy when we fall in love, when we marry, when we find a great job, when we have children, and when our children succeed. Much of what we say makes us happy involves getting what we want—either materialistically or in terms of what we want life and the universe to provide for us.

In between these events, we settle for less-than-happy days when we yearn for and often work toward more money, a new mate, a better job, a new car, a sexier body, or the next vacation, or perhaps we are waiting for our marriage, children, career, or health to get back on track. The relative balance between these periods of having what we want and waiting for it constitutes what I refer to as *ordinary happiness.* It is not a bad way to live. There is nothing horrible or deplorable about it. In fact, you can get quite good at it, maximizing the good times and minimizing the bad. It definitely leads to some happiness. But what few believe—the secret that Tibetan monk revealed to me that Saturday afternoon in Virginia—is that *more is possible.* But before we go there, I want you to take a moment to identify your approach to ordinary happiness.

EXERCISE: EXPLORING ORDINARY HAPPINESS

Download worksheet at www.mindfulnessforchocolate.com.

Sources of Happiness: *Set a timer for sixty seconds and list the first ten things that come to mind that make you happy and/or would make you happy.*

1.   6.
2.   7.
3.   8.
4.   9.
5.   10.

Themes: Sources of Happiness

- **Circle** the items that require *you* to do something different (e.g., go back to school, move).
- Put an **asterisk (*)** next to the items that require *another person to do something* (e.g., get hired, propose) for you to be happy.
- Put an **X** next to items that require the *universe or society to change or rely on chance* (e.g., win the lottery, meet Mr./Miss Right, change a law, stock market change, etc.).

Threats to Happiness: *List the first ten things that are the greatest impediments to experiencing happiness more regularly.*

1.   6.
2.   7.
3.   8.
4.   9.
5.   10.

Themes: Threats to Happiness

- **Circle** the items that involve you to *do or not do something* (e.g., fail an exam, manage money poorly, etc.).
- Put an **asterisk (*)** next to the items that involve the *actions of another person* (e.g., someone says or does something hurtful, get fired, etc.).
- Put an **X** next to something that involves the *universe, society, or chance events disrupting your happiness* (e.g., stock market crash, death of loved one, etc.).

Evaluation: How many of the items on your lists require:	**Sources of Happiness**	**Threats to Happiness**
You to do something different		
Another person to do something different		
The universe/situation to change		

Source of Happiness: Based on this exercise, what do you tend to rely most on for happiness?

☐ Yourself ☐ Others ☐ Life circumstances

As you read further and learn more about positive psychology, the significance of your analysis to the above questions will make more sense. However, suffice it to say that the more you focus on actions and factors that you control to make you happier, the happier you are likely to be. If you are sitting around waiting for others or life to change in order to make you happy, you are more likely to be disappointed.

POSITIVE PSYCHOLOGY: THE SCIENCE OF HAPPINESS

A newer branch of psychology scientifically investigates happiness: positive psychology. By surveying, observing, and interviewing people, positive psychologists study how people seek happiness and what is important and unimportant in the pursuit of happiness. In addition to identifying correlates of happiness, these psychologists also explore ways to increase the quality and quantity of happiness in people's lives. The findings of researchers such as Martin Seligman, author of *Authentic Happiness*,[1] and Alan Carr, author of *Positive Psychology*,[2] are often surprising, contradicting many common assumptions about what leads to happiness. These discoveries highlight many of the traps that keep people stuck, settling for ordinary happiness. Correcting these mistaken myths about happiness is the first step to finding it.

MYTH NO. 1: MORE MONEY
LEADS TO GREATER HAPPINESS

Closer to the truth: having enough money to meet your basic needs and afford some luxury conveniences is more likely to result in happiness than significant wealth.

Perhaps one of the more startling findings of positive psychology is that money does not have a direct correlation to happiness. Once a person's basic needs are met—food, shelter, clothing—and they have enough for some luxury conveniences, more money brings negligibly more happiness. In fact, in a worldwide study, researchers found that happiness peaks at an income of $100,000 and begins to reverse at $250,000, with variations by region, with more pricier regions like New York and California requiring a bit more to thrive.[3] Thus the wealthy are *not* more likely to be significantly happier than people with a more moderate income in the same society, as celebrity news regularly documents. Even more unexpectedly, even though the overall real income has risen dramatically in prosperous nations during the past fifty years, the average level of happiness and life satisfaction has not.

Dr. Ed Diener at the University of Illinois and colleagues at the Gallup Organization provide more nuanced analysis of the situation.[4] Using the Gallup World Poll, the first representative sample of the planet earth, they analyzed the effects of wealth on life satisfaction versus positive emotions, such as happiness. Whereas income that allowed for higher standards of living and conveniences predicted positive evaluations of one's life (i.e., life satisfaction), positive emotions such as happiness were associated with fulfillment of psychological needs such as autonomy, respect, learning, using one's skills, and having social support.

In one of my favorite research studies ever, Dr. Quoidbach and his colleagues in Europe and Canada provided the first direct evidence that having wealth—in fact, just thinking about wealth—likely *impairs* a person's ability to savor positive experiences and emotions.[5] In the first half of the study, all wealthier individuals reported lower savoring abilities in their everyday lives than those with lower incomes. Additionally, non-wealthy individuals who were given a prompt to think about wealth (literally a photo of a stack of bills) experienced a similar impairment in savoring. In the second part of the study (and, no, I didn't pay them to do this), the participants were given a piece of chocolate either with or without exposure to the reminder of wealth. Both wealthy and less wealthy participants enjoyed their chocolate more *without* the reminder of wealth.

Curious about what does promote happiness in affluent countries, Dr. Jan Delhey, a German social scientist, analyzed the most recent World Values Study from forty-eight countries, including poor agrarian and rich postindustrial societies.[6] The analysis revealed a consistent pattern of postmaterialist concerns—defined as personal autonomy and job creativity—as predictors of happiness in wealthier countries in contrast to poorer countries.

When *does* money make a difference? A recent boost in pay or winning the lottery does correlate to more happiness—but only for the two or three months that follow. After that, most return to their former level of happiness. Curiously, many who win the lottery are actually *less* happy and some even suicidal one to two years later. What seems to matter more than money itself is how you *view* money. Those who value money more than other life goals and pursuits are consistently *less* happy than others with their levels of income and their lives in general. Thus, *materialism* and valuing money seem to create less happiness.

MYTH NO. 2: MORE PLEASURE BRINGS GREATER HAPPINESS

Closer to the truth: avoiding habituation to pleasures increases happiness.

A large proportion of our financial resources go to seeking pleasure: a great meal, passionate sex, beautiful clothes, a good concert, a piece of art, a comfortable home, a sophisticated car, extreme sports, and of course, chocolate. In fact, much of the average person's existence is dedicated to seeking pleasure. Why? Pleasures are characterized by instant and almost effortless positive emotion. Instant and guaranteed happiness! By doing X, we are relatively sure we will feel happy.

The problem is that happiness derived from pleasure cannot last. At some point we must stop eating, an orgasm ends, clothes go out of style, and our home and car need repair. Even if we could find a way to create a balanced diet eating primarily chocolate, there is the problem of *habituation*. The body is programmed to habituate to any external stimulus. For example, when you first bring a fragrant bouquet into a room, the room is filled with an incredible scent that is delicious to drink in. However, within ten minutes of being in the room, you are not likely to even notice the scent. Your nose has sent an endless number of messages to the brain saying, "Smells like flowers," and the brain has said, "Yes, I know. They are lovely." But the brain no longer focuses or notices these messages from the nose to make room for *new* information coming in. In this case, leaving the room and coming back would offer *new* information, and you would notice the scent disappearing as you leave and reappearing as you enter the room again. Otherwise, you would need to add more or different flowers to get the brain to say, "Hey, there is something else good around here."

Thus, whether the pleasure we seek is through food, sex, chocolate, possessions, or entertainment, after a certain amount of stimulation we need more or different stimulation for it to be pleasurable. That's how we end up on what positive psychologist Martin Seligman refers to as the *hedonistic treadmill*: the never-ending search for the next pleasure (and one of my favorite terms in all of psychology). Although this treadmill is good for corporations, marketers, and economies, it is one of the most common happiness traps of the modern age.

In a recent study, Dr. Julian House and colleagues at the University of Toronto identified even bigger problems that come along with jumping on the hedonistic treadmill, which typically includes an impatient desire for more.[7] When examining the effects of immediate gratification and impatience on happiness, they found that simply exposing people to fast food impeded their ability to experience happiness from both pictures of natural beauty and beautiful music, indicating that the more time one spends on the treadmill the more likely one is to forget to smell the roses.

One possible exception that Drs. Alba and Williams noted when comparing the past thirty years of studies on hedonistic consumerism and pleasure is the purchase of objects versus experiences: having versus doing.[8] Some evidence suggests that paying money for pleasurable experiences—taking a ride in a hot air balloon, going to a concert, or taking a vacation—seem to have a slower rate of adaption and thus a longer period of enjoyment compared to buying a favorite gadget, car, or outfit. This may be because an experience that leaves no tangible evidence exists primarily in a person's mind. They posit that these experiences may become more positive and relived over time when the person shares the experience with others or replays it in his or her mind.

MYTH NO. 3: FULFILLING YOUR DREAMS BRINGS HAPPINESS

Closer to the truth: actively pursuing dreams increases happiness; achieving them does not affect happiness for very long.

Often, we assume that when we achieve life goals and ambitions—completing a degree, getting a job, earning an award or recognition, getting married, having a child, buying a dream home—that we will be happier. Positive psychologists have also found that fulfilling a life goal does not lead to greater happiness (you do have to wonder why they call them "positive" with research findings like this). In many ways, achieving these goals works similarly to seeking pleasure. In the first few months following successfully achieving a major life goal, people report being happier than before. However, afterward the achievement becomes the norm, and we go back to our prior level of happiness.

There is some evidence that making progress toward achieving goals is more likely to promote happiness than the final achievement, possibly related to the adage that anticipation is often better than realization. In their analysis of research on the subject, Drs. Hannah Klug and Günter Maier at Bielefeld University in Germany found that a person's subjective well-being is higher when pursuing a goal versus attaining a goal and that this relationship is stronger in individualist cultures.[9] They note that if achieving a goal does not lead to a clear new goal, the goal attainment is likely to be accompanied by a sense of emptiness, which likely accounts for the drop in happiness. Similarly, in longitudinal research on happiness, researchers at George Mason University in Virginia found that goal attainment only gave a three-month boost in happiness, whereas gratitude and a sense of life purpose are more likely to reduce depression.[10]

The one notable exception to this may be marriage. Positive psychologists have found that married people generally report being happier than unmarried or divorced people. However, an international study using American, British, and German data conducted by Bruce Chapman and Cahit Guven from the Australian National University found that being unhappily married is correlated with less happiness than being happily married, divorced, or single, especially for women.[11] They found no causal link between happiness and marriage, meaning having a happy disposition did not predict getting married. They did find that happier people are more likely to stay single rather than be unhappily married. So, as most married people already know, marriage does not come with a happiness guarantee, but happily married is happier than average.

MYTH NO. 4: NEGATIVE EMOTIONS REDUCE HAPPINESS

Closer to the truth: in-the-moment positive emotions are closely related to happiness.

It would seem logical that those who report more anger, sadness, and other negative emotions would be less happy. Thankfully, logic and good reason have never stopped scientists from being skeptical and asking more questions. Researchers have reported some surprising results. It turns out that having more negative emotions does *not* mean you have proportionately less happiness. The inverse is also true: If you experience a lot of positive emotions, this does not mean that you will be less likely to experience negative emotions. For example, Dr. Michael Cohn and colleagues measured the emotions of eighty-six college students daily for a month and found that negative emotions did not interfere with the benefits of their positive emotions.[12] In their study, they also found that in-the-moment positive emotions—rather than general positive evaluations of one's life—were associated with happiness and desirable life outcome.

The interesting twist in understanding positive and negative emotions is gender. Apparently, women are more likely to experience more of both positive *and* negative emotions. They experience more happiness and joy as well as more sadness and anger. At this point, it is not clear whether this is due to biological factors, social factors, or simply their greater willingness to report emotions to researchers. However, it does appear that experiencing greater happiness may involve an equivalent ability to feel less desired emotions, such as sadness and anger.

MYTH NO. 5: BEING HEALTHY INCREASES HAPPINESS

Closer to the truth: health significantly affects happiness only if you suffer from five or more ailments.

Both of my grandmothers always said that the most important thing in life is one's health. Although this adage is repeated continually in my family and is one of the few things all generations seem to agree upon (along with the value of a good dessert), positive psychologists have found otherwise. It turns out that *objective* good health—how a panel of doctors might describe our health—is not correlated with happiness. Instead, it is our *subjective* view—what we think of our own health—that is correlated with happiness. Researchers have found that severely ill cancer patients differ only slightly in global level of happiness and that those with a severe and long-term disability generally do not differ unless they have five or more serious problems. These findings highlight the resilience and the ability of humans to adapt to life circumstances even when the body is in pain and ill.

HAPPINESS AS A LIFE SKILL

When it comes to research on happiness, Buddhists have been studying it a bit longer than positive psychologists: The difference is approximately twenty-five hundred years compared to thirty. Apparently, humans have not changed all that much; both report similar findings. Having a bit more time to reflect on the paradoxes of humans and happiness, Buddhists have developed a unique spin on happiness: They view it as an *action*, rather than a feeling or emotion. They see themselves as actively *practicing* it rather than finding or creating it in their lives. Matthieu Ricard, a native Frenchman who now practices Buddhism at his primary residence in Nepal, describes the Buddhist approach to happiness as a *skill*.[13] In the West, we tend to see that we can *work toward* or *seek out* happiness, viewing it as a "thing" out there in the world that we must find, discover, or earn. In marked contrast, the Buddhist approach is to see it as a *verb*: something one does.

For most of us, this is a radical new way to think about happiness. You do not have to wait for the dream lover, perfect job, ideal weight, desired salary, good luck, right timing, or anything else. You do not have to *have* anything to be happy. Instead, it is a thing that you *do* and therefore can choose to engage in during virtually any moment of your life. As you may have guessed by now, this book is designed to help you learn this important life skill.

The New Formula for Happiness

Let's compare the old and new formulas for happiness:

The New Formula for Happiness

	Happiness Equals =	*Underlying Process*
Ordinary Happiness	"Getting what I want"	External world conforms to my wishes
Extraordinary Happiness (or Joy)	A "learned skill" that becomes a *habit*	Internal world shapes external experience

This new formula has radical implications for those of us who have organized our personal and professional lives around devising plans to get what we want in order to be happy. Many of us have spent countless hours, days, and even years working for what we want so we can finally find or achieve happiness. Similarly, some of us have spent countless hours, days, and years being crushed and depressed because we have not been able to find or create what we think we need to be happy. Certainly, the most industrialized economies are fueled by our attempts to purchase what we think will bring us happiness.

Ordinary happiness is dependent on the external world operating according to our personal plans and wishes. In contrast, our newer understanding of happiness is that it is dependent on one's attitude toward life: it is a habit of thinking, doing, and being. When life is going well, there may not be a huge difference between the old and new formulas for happiness. The difference between the two becomes clear when the external world stops conforming to one's wishes. That is when we see the real distinction between ordinary and extraordinary happiness. Ordinary happiness comes and goes each time the wind and other external circumstances change; extraordinary happiness endures regardless of the weather.

Try as we might to buy and control the external world, we ultimately cannot control others, forces of nature, and the ordering of the universe. I know. I tried for years, read a lot of books, and still could not do it. As a therapist, I have also worked with thousands of others who found that this approach ultimately fails, even if it seems to work well for years or decades at a time. Ultimately, the ones we love will die; people choose cruelty over kindness; something delays your best plans; and all the money in the world does not buy authentic love and affection. So, at some point, it makes sense to try a new approach to happiness to see if it works any better than trying to control the uncontrollable.

The following exercise will get you started by identifying where and how you already have started to cultivate elements of extraordinary happiness in your life.

EXERCISE: FIRST STEPS TO EXTRAORDINARY HAPPINESS

Download worksheet at www.mindfulnessforchocolate.com.

Part I: Future Visions

Take a moment to imagine yourself living a typical day in a state of joy or extraordinary happiness. Envision going through the most difficult moments of the day without external circumstances dampening your sense of joy. Describe how your behaviors and attitudes are different:

- In your daily routine: _____
- In your emotional life: _____
- In your personal and social life: _____
- In your working/educational life: _____
- In your spiritual life: _____
- Who do you think will support and encourage you? How will you ensure that you stay connected to these people? _____
- Who do you think will be less supportive and encouraging? How will you interact with these people to keep you moving in a positive direction? _____

Part II: Take Action

Based on this exercise, what three small things can you start doing today that would move you toward extraordinary happiness?

1. _____
2. _____
3. _____

• 3 •

Chocolate Is a Vegetable

Mapping the Truths You Live By

$\mathcal{A}$ccording to the U.S. Department of Agriculture's Food Guide Pyramid categorization and my high school biology teacher, the cocoa bean is a vegetable, or more accurately a legume, making it a close relative to one of the few vegetables I have not befriended: the lima bean. Yet most of us fail to keep chocolate's origin in mind and instead attach more complex and convoluted meanings. For many, chocolate is half savior and half demon. It saves us from our daily stresses, rewards us for good behavior, and helps us celebrate our joys and accomplishments. Yet at the same time, it is our enemy when it comes to managing our weight and nourishing our bodies well, generating a disquieting mix of gratification and anxiety with every bite. This "guilty pleasure" view of chocolate permeates society to such an extent that the fact that chocolate is healthy has become newsworthy material in recent years. Like many other foods made primarily from vegetables, chocolate is rich in antioxidants, particularly flavonoids and catechins, helping to fight heart disease and cancer. But for those who remember that chocolate is derived primarily from a vegetable—despite the constant clamor about its evils—the health benefits do not come as a surprise.

Our losing sight of chocolate's true origin parallels much of what happens in our relationship to life's most inescapable realities, including the limits of physics and chemistry, the fundamental dynamics of human relationships, and existential certainties. Both with chocolate and life, basic truths are obscured by social myths and dominant opinions. The voices of others tell us how life *should* work and what *should* make us happy, drowning out many of the simple truths that we know and/ or regularly observe in our daily lives. When we lose sight of obvious truths, we tend to get confused and create more turmoil and problems than are necessary. This is what happens for many of us in our search for happiness. The key is to become more aware of the maps we use to define and seek happiness.

MAPPING YOUR WAY TO HAPPINESS

What is the difference between ordinary and extraordinary happiness? How do you arrive at one rather than another? As a psychotherapist—and a human being traveling the same journey as everyone else on this planet—I have come to notice that people who live lives of extraordinary happiness have different maps than those living more ordinarily happy lives. By "map," I am referring to the following assumptions:

- Assumption No. 1: your beliefs about how the universe works
- Assumption No. 2: your beliefs about your role in the universe
- Assumption No. 3: your beliefs about how one goes about finding happiness given Assumptions No. 1 and No. 2 above

You may ask, does it really matter what I *believe* about how the universe is constructed and how happiness fits in? And the answer is: most definitely! What you think—and unconsciously assume—about how the universe works has everything to do with whether or not you find happiness and whether it is ordinary or extraordinary.

Typically, we do not consciously construct our maps to happiness. Instead, we haphazardly piece them together as we watch others, beginning with our parents and teachers and later our friends and peers, and listen to the stories of others, whether a fairytale, novel, tabloid, movie, or our dad's favorite story. Each person we observe and each story we hear—whether an example of happiness or disappointment—becomes a piece of a puzzle that we use to construct our map. When we hear about a vacation, wedding, purchase, or dinner menu of someone we believe to be happy, we are apt to put this in our map as a possible avenue to happiness if we believe the source to be credible. When we hear stories of how ruin and despair occur in someone's life, we put that in our map as something to avoid.

Our maps are more like puzzles that get put together one piece at a time, and sometimes adding one piece necessitates reorganizing all the others. Often this is a good thing. When most of us were teenagers, we had the idea that if we got the right look and had the right "stuff" (cars, clothes, makeup, gadgets, etc.), we would be cool enough to attract the love, money, and careers of our dreams. Eventually and thankfully, most of us discover that most of that "stuff" is not a stable road to happiness, and so we rearrange our maps—often relegating "stuff" to a lesser priority in the search for happiness. In fact, an entire school of psychotherapy, narrative therapy, was developed specifically to help people examine the stories that create, augment, and/or exacerbate their pain by consciously choosing which parts to keep and which parts need editing. Obviously more complex than simply revising a story on paper, rewriting the typically unconscious stories we live by can be done with some thoughtful intervention. This chapter is all about helping you to rearrange your map so that you find a more direct and stable route to happiness.

EXERCISE: EXAMINING YOUR MAP FOR HAPPINESS

Download worksheet at www.mindfulnessforchocolate.com.

Where Have You Been?

First, let's examine what has brought you happiness and unhappiness over the years.

1. Identify reliable *internal factors* that have contributed most to your *happiness* as a child and now (attitude, thoughts, behaviors): _____

2. Identify reliable *external factors* that have contributed most to your *happiness* as a child and now (others, places, situations, etc.): _____

3. Identify reliable *internal factors* that have contributed most to your <u>unhappiness</u> as a child and now (attitude, thoughts, behaviors): _____

4. Identify reliable *external factors* that have contributed most to your <u>unhappiness</u> as a child and now (others, places, situations, etc.): _____

Guiding Principles

Let's examine your beliefs about happiness and unhappiness

1. To be truly happy, I need—at minimum—the following five things in my life:
   1.
   2.
   3.
   4.
   5.

2. What three things do you believe are key to finding happiness?

    1.
    2.
    3.

3. What three things are most likely to cause unhappiness?

    1.
    2.
    3.

4. Why do you believe you are not happier more often?

_____

Reflecting on Your Map

1. Identify three common themes (getting what you want, getting away from daily life, high points in life, etc.):

    1.
    2.
    3.

2. What type of external factors tend to be essential for your happiness (being in a certain place, with a person, achieving a goal)?

_____

3. What type of internal factors tend to be critical for your happiness (attitudes, beliefs, behaviors, etc.)?

_____

4. Are you doing what you know you need to do to create happiness in your life? How so, or why not?

_____

5. What are your greatest obstacles to happiness and how do you deal with them?

_____

COSMIC MAPS AND EXTRAORDINARY HAPPINESS

Your assumptions about how the universe works determine where and how you go about seeking happiness in this life. Philosophers refer to some of these foundational assumptions as our ontology and epistemology, but it might be simpler to refer to them as "cosmic maps." Rarely do we take the time to reflect on these basic assumptions that guide our lives in intimate ways. By doing so, I think we will become much clearer about what we are seeking and why.

GETTING THERE: TREASURE VERSUS ROAD MAPS

One of the most obvious differences between maps that lead to ordinary versus extraordinary happiness is whether they can be characterized as treasure maps or road maps. Treasure maps reveal where someone else has hidden something of great worth that you get to keep if you can find it. Typically, there is a game or trickery involved: obstacles must be overcome, riddles solved, and dangers avoided. When it comes to treasure maps, there is only one right answer. Many times, competition is involved, and you must be the first to find the treasure. The mapmaker is generally not kind but smugly watching as you stumble, get off track, or get lost.

A road map, on the other hand, has no objective or goal. Instead, it is a tool that is reused time and again to help you move from point to point. The mapmaker makes no promises other than that he or she will try to help you to get where you want to go—certainly less exciting but more user friendly over the long haul.

When your cosmic map looks more like a treasure map, you see yourself in relationship to the universe, cosmos, or divine in a way that is similar to the treasure seeker and the treasure mapmaker. The universe is seen as a force that doles out goodies if you can successfully play the game. The universe is usually not on your side; rather, you need to get on its side or at least agree to play by its rules. In contrast, when you view your cosmic map as a road map, you develop a very different relationship to the universe. In this case, the universe is simply trying to offer useful information to help you on your way. It is educating you, showing you "what is" rather than trying to get you to a certain destination. So, the first step is to know whether you are using a treasure or road map. It will determine whether you end up finding ordinary or extraordinary happiness.

TREASURE MAPS: THE UNIVERSE AS GIFT GIVER

Treasure maps view the universe or God as "gift giver" and therefore lead to ordinary forms of happiness—or worse, if you are unsuccessful in finding the treasure. The idea is this: "If I am good and follow the rules, I will be duly rewarded." Most of us are handed such a map as a child—based on a simple interpretation of our community's or religion's rules—in order to promote good behavior. The premise is this: if you lie, cheat, and steal, God/parents/adults will punish you, but if you are good, you will be rewarded. However, there is ample evidence that the universe does not work this way. In fact, many of the kindest people who have walked the planet—Jesus, Gandhi, Dalai Lama, Mother Teresa, Mandela, Martin Luther King Jr., Buddha, to name a few—were not consistently rewarded with an easy life, nor was their compassion regularly returned with reciprocal kindness. Clearly, sainthood does not guarantee a happy or easy life. Yet many of us keep trying to do the right thing in hope of being rewarded with a happy life.

When we strive to treat others well, give extra time at the office, are generous with our time, money, and heart, we generally expect things to go well. It seems logical that others will naturally *want* to treat us in kind and appreciate our efforts. Unfortunately, this is not always the case. (If you have been on the planet a while, I am sure you may have a few examples to prove my point.) Living a life guided by a generous spirit and a kind heart reduces certain types of problems, such as conflict with others, but it does not necessitate a stress-free life or stress-free relations with others. Thus when a problem arises, people who have universe-as-gift-giver as part of their cosmic maps have two problems to deal with: (1) the initial problem, and (2) anger that the problem occurred—because according to their maps, it should not have. The secondary problem is simply a result of using a particular cosmic map; thankfully, we have other options.

ROAD MAPS: DIVINE AS INSTRUCTOR

When you use your cosmic map as a road map, you interact with it— and therefore life, God, and the universe—in a very different way. The universe in this scenario can be seen as instructive about how life works: either in a neutral sense (it is just a map of what is) or a positive sense (this map is intended to be helpful). In my work with clients, I have seen people use both of these road maps to move productively toward extraordinary happiness.

Some, such as traditional Buddhists, atheists, and scientists, use the neutral road map: The universe is viewed as neutral and benign. For example, traditional Buddhists do not believe the Buddha is there to guide them or make life easy for them. Instead, the Buddha was a teacher about life truths, which is summarized as "life just is what it is." The universe just is. People are what they are. Even the cocoa bean is seen for what it is—a legume. Their map instructs them to open their hearts and minds to acknowledge what is right in front of them. When good things happen— you get the job you want, you find the love of your life, a stranger offers much-needed help—you are grateful and compassionate. When challenges come—you lose your job, the love of your life leaves you, a person cuts you off in traffic—you acknowledge how you are feeling and soften toward the source of your suffering but never fall into feeling like a victim because there is no one and nothing to blame. A person holding this neutral perspective acknowledges that challenges and difficulties are part of life and, therefore, does not go into "victim" mode thinking, such as "It's unfair that my boss did not appreciate me; something is wrong with her." Or, "It's unfair that my spouse left me because I have been loyal and loving." Or, "That person is a horrible driver and should have his license taken away." Instead, they accept that they are being educated on all possible happenings on the journey of life and are open to whatever may happen.

The other type of road map is used to view whatever is happening as a "gift" or "lesson." This approach, typically used by most Christians, some Buddhists, and most New Age thinkers, assumes that there is an *intelligent* and *benevolent* force that organizes the universe. Thus any challenge or difficulty comes from this divine intelligence, and therefore there is something for us to learn or grow from. As Pema Chödrön, an American Buddhist, so eloquently explains: "This very moment is the perfect teacher."[1] To my knowledge, there is no scientific evidence to prove this theory, but I have noticed in my practice as a psychotherapist that such an attitude—or even the more conservative belief in a neutral universe—greatly reduces suffering and allows a person to live with more joy, hope, and happiness. To further help on this journey, in *Finding Your Own North Star*, Martha Beck describes how to use the inner "compass" of your essential selves to more easily and directly navigate toward your divinely destined place of joy.[2] She proposes that we each have an inner sense of divinely informed guidance, which we experience through strong emotions (both positive and negative), bodily reactions, and intuition.

So, at this point, the real question becomes a question of utility: *Is your map working for you? Will it work for you when tragedy strikes?* Would adopting a benign or positive view of the universe help you to respond to problems more gracefully and live a happier life?

Personally, I have found the universe-as-instructor map helpful in many areas of my life. Most frequently, I use it while driving around town, but this also applies to those who get around with rapid transit or those who frequently find themselves helplessly waiting for anything. In Los Angeles, people generally drive as fast as traffic conditions allow. I assume this results in an average speed that is close to the posted limits. But now and then, I encounter people who are driving considerably under the speed limit for no apparent reason. This is especially problematic when there are only one or two lanes. There was a time in my life where I would find these slow drivers quite irritating. But one day I decided to see what would happen if I saw this as a lesson, and I had the most remarkable insight: slow drivers teach me to slow down the pace of my life. By no means am I a speed demon on the road, but I do like to keep things moving with exceptional precision. My new view of slow drivers as my teachers has brought much more peace into my life than my prior view of things. On a good day, I silently send them a thank you and see them as a gift sent to remind me to be mindful. On days when I am feeling less noble because I am running late, I notice the lesson and jokingly say aloud, "Yes, God, I know I have once again overbooked my day, but can you please send me the lesson tomorrow? I am in a bit of a rush with important places to go." And I laugh—at myself.

Exercise: Your Cosmic Map

Download worksheet at www.mindfulnessforchocolate.com.

The following questions can help you identify what you believe about life and how things work. Identify your basic belief and then how it informs how you respond to difficult times (if at all).

	Basic Belief	How This Belief Affects How I Handle Challenges
Who/what organized the universe (God, nature, etc.)?		
Why did they/it organize it? What is the purpose of life?		
How do you believe human life fits into the universe? Is there anything beyond this life?		

	Basic Belief	How This Belief Affects How I Handle Challenges
Do our actions in this life affect anything that comes after? How? Why?		
Do we have responsibilities in this life to something larger than ourselves? How? Why?		
Why do bad things happen to good people?		
Are there any sayings or principles that guide your life choices (e.g., Golden Rule, follow your heart, etc.)?		

TRUSTING THE MAPMAKER: SURRENDER

Another noticeable difference between people who use treasure maps and road maps is the level of trust the user puts in the mapmaker. If you are using a treasure map, it is clear that the mapmaker is not your ally, and in many cases, the mapmaker's intentions are questionable at best. After all, if the mapmaker was a straight shooter, you would have been given some hints, told the purchase price, or simply handed the treasure. In contrast, when you are handed a road map, it is easier to trust that the mapmaker has your best interests at heart. The idea is that they are giving you the best and most accurate information they have to help you on your journey.

There is tremendous peace that comes with trusting that the universe and/or God is not out to get you—but actually to help you. When you fully trust that this is the case, even when the hard times come, you are able to trust even if you have come to the end of the road and see no way to go on. For those who enjoy TED Talks (www.ted.com), you can find numerous examples of how this works by viewing talks on the following topics: "death," "disability," "failure," and/or "race" (visit www.mindfulnessforchocolatelovers.com for recommendations). That is what is sometimes referred to as *surrender*: believing that whatever is happening is part of some divine, cosmic plan or lesson and that everything will be OK even if it seems there is no way it could be.

Exercise: Treasure vs. Road Map Quiz

Download worksheet at www.mindfulnessforchocolate.com.

For each pair below, give yourself one point *in the corresponding column for the statement that best describes how you think.*

1 or 0	Treasure-Map Thinking: Column No. 1	Road-Map Thinking: Column No. 2	1 or 0
	Disappointment is hard for me.	I handle disappointment well.	
	I am good at getting what I want.	I am good at enjoying whatever comes my way.	
	I am often angry or hurt when others criticize me.	I handle criticism well.	
	I feel that I am in control of my life and/or, at times, out of control of my life.	I feel that there is a plan for my life OR there is no need to plan—it will come.	
	It is important that I feel appreciated by others for my efforts.	I am not strongly motivated by the appreciation of others.	
	It really bothers me when life is unfair to me and/or others.	When life is unfair, I make peace with what happened quickly.	
	Everyone is free to seek happiness his/her own way.	Happiness is a choice.	
	← **Total Points Column No. 1**	**Total Points Column No. 2 →**	

If your Column No. 1 score is larger than No. 2, SUBTRACT Column No. 2 Score from No. 1; plot on the LEFT half of scale below.
If your Column No. 2 score is larger than No. 1, SUBTRACT Column No. 1 Score from No. 2; plot on the right half of scale.

Treasure Map 7———5———3———0———3———5———7 **Road Map**

Small Steps in a Better Direction

Identify three situations where it would most benefit your life to let go of "treasure map" mentality (e.g., your relationship with your spouse; your career path, etc.).

1. _____

2. _____

3. _____

Identify one thing you could do in each of these areas to make a small change toward seeing life as a road map.

1. _____

2. _____

3. _____

WHERE ARE YOU GOING?
DESTINATION PARADISE OR JOYRIDE?

Perhaps the greatest difference between those who have maps that lead to ordinary versus extraordinary happiness is understanding where they are going. Ordinary maps to happiness identify their destination: paradise. They believe that they can use their cosmic map to achieve their goals, seek their dreams, and find lasting happiness. But we all know—well, most do—that there is no such utopia or place that offers unending peace, joy, and happiness without effort or input on our part. Yet, upon closer inspection, most of our maps contain such fantasies and dreams, which often take the form of a paradise-generating relationship, child, job, house, large paycheck, or lifestyle.

In contrast, those who discover extraordinary happiness use their maps differently. There is no such final destination. There is no predetermined or preferred goal. Instead, they are out for a *joyride*. What does that mean? They get in their cars—perhaps with a destination in mind or perhaps without one—but they are able to go where the road takes them, even if it was not in their original plans. They see detours as new adventures and traffic delays as part of what happens when you get out on the open road. They are aware that no matter what happens on one road, there are an endless number of other paths to follow. So, no matter where the journey takes them, they are able to have fun, laugh, and recognize that it is part of being on any excursion worth taking. The key to joyriding is knowing the difference between pleasure and happiness.

JOYRIDING: DISTINGUISHING
PLEASURE FROM HAPPINESS

Cosmic maps that lead to ordinary happiness are easily recognized by this one feature: confusing pleasure and happiness. The two have become

synonymous in modern culture. "I am happy when I feel good." But pleasure and happiness are two very different things. Happiness is an emotion,
whereas pleasure is a sensory experience. Our culture is obsessed with sex,
food, gadgets, and entertainment—all are forms of pleasure. They make us
feel good, but this feeling begins with the body, not the heart.

Is pleasure bad? No. It is just confusing. The instant gratification
that characterizes pleasure makes it harder to make choices that lead
to greater forms of happiness. When posed with the option, most will
choose a relationship or sex with anybody rather than face loneliness, a
good or not-so-good movie rather than taking time for meditation and
prayer, television over organizing a cluttered closet, or chocolate over
lima beans. The problem is that, over time, such choices can lead to
situations that detract from our lives rather than bring greater happiness,
which explains why many religious traditions recommend strictly limit-
ing various forms of pleasure.

Most monastic traditions, including Christian and Buddhist, have
reduced the number of earthly pleasures for those seeking more spiritual
lives. Many have taken this to mean that pleasures such as sex, alcohol,
and "the finer things" are sins and obstacles on the spiritual path and even
barriers to a spiritual life. Some would argue that this is the case. I would
say that the issue is not so black and white. Pleasures are *distractions* that
make it harder to find true happiness. They lure us off our path. Would
you rather (A) watch television and eat ice cream or (B) work out after a
long day at the office? For most, option A is more appealing: it involves
the most pleasure. But science is very clear that the latter option is the
most likely to lead to long-term happiness. A blanket denial of all pleasure
makes it easier to make the choices that lead to long-term happiness. This
may be a good way to begin making new choices, but in the long run
denying all pleasures has the same effect as indulging pleasure: missing
the target for extraordinary happiness. The approach of denial—although
often a useful tool along the path at various points—results in a rigid and
fear-based approach to life, rather than a joy-filled one.

IT IS *HOW* YOU TRAVEL, NOT WHERE

A mentor once told me: "There is one in every class." I have since
repeated this truth to many of the younger faculty I supervise. As a

university professor, I work hard and always go the extra mile for my students, but my colleague's sage advice is true. No matter how hard I try or how far out of my way I go, typically there is one person in every class who is less than satisfied and thinks I should have done it differently—which means I have a choice. I can choose to be disappointed that I did not receive perfect evaluations from my students— that I did not arrive at the destination I hoped for—or I can focus on teaching well—the *how* of my work. Over the years, I have come to realize that I cannot make every student totally satisfied, because each student has unique and contradictory needs. Some need more theory, others more examples, and still others more experiential exercises. All I can do is listen to each student's needs and consider these in the context of the demands of the class and my students' long-term professional growth. My satisfaction with my work must come from *how* I teach rather than whether I am popular. Ironically—or not so ironically—once I accepted this fact and stopped trying to make everyone happier, I became a better instructor. Living a life of extraordinary happiness follows a similar principle.

As you begin to shift your focus from the destination to the journey, the *how* of living becomes your focus. The question shifts to "How do I meaningfully work toward what I want?" and away from "How do I get what I want?" This shift is countercultural in the West, which makes the pursuit of getting what you want a primary motivator and goal. However, when the focus of each journey is integrity and meaning, each step is satisfying and rewarding. You no longer determine success based on whether you end up at your intended destination or not. Instead, you judge your choices and conduct—over which you have full control—and ask if you approve of them. If you do, the journey was a success, and since you always have control over your thoughts and behaviors, even the greatest "failure" can be a major personal success.

Over the years, I have worked with hundreds of couples who are on the brink of separating or divorcing. Often I am asked, "Is it even worth trying to salvage this relationship? It feels so hopeless." Unless there are clear indications of violence or similar issues, I always answer, "Yes." I say yes because in the big scheme of things, *how* they decided to stay together or part ways is more important than whether they ultimately stay together. Most times, one or both partners are focused solely on staying together—anything else would be "failure." But consider a shift in focus to the following: "How am I treating my partner, myself, and others during this difficult time?" "Am I acting with integrity even when I feel angry and hurt?" "Can I still show caring even if I do not feel 'in love' with my partner?" "Can I still respect my partner and myself as human beings?" When the focus shifts to how you treat the other and yourself rather than simply staying together, it is a different process. No matter what the outcome in terms of living arrangements, partners who make this shift have a sense of peace in *how* the decision was made and who each person was in the process. The ironic twist is that I have found that most couples who can shift to focusing on *how* they are struggling in their relationship are able to stay together because respect and caring take precedence over getting what they want.

Exercise: From Seeking Paradise to Going for a Joyride

Download worksheet at www.mindfulnessforchocolate.com.

How do you go about achieving happiness in your life?

	Destination Paradise *Describe your goal and how you have tried to get what you want in the past.*	Joyride *Describe one way you can be more focused on the HOW of the journey toward these goals.*
Example: weight loss	*Losing weight by strict dieting; regaining it all; dieting again*	*Changing focus to eating right and exercising to be healthy*
Personal Physical and emotional health; identity; self-esteem		
Relationships Significant other, children, parents, friends, coworkers		
Career/Education Career decisions; attitude toward work		
Spiritual Spiritual practice; time for reflection, etc.		
Financial/Everyday Stuff Managing finances; daily routine and stressors		

WHO'S GOING? TRAVELING SOLO OR BY CARAVAN?

Who do you stay connected with? And why? When you look at the maps of those who experience more extraordinary forms of happiness, you see a pattern: they are connected—to family, friends, and their community. The Buddhists refer to the special group of people who help you on your spiritual journey as your *sangha*. Traditionally the sangha is led by a Buddhist monk, nun, or official of some sort, but in a more informal practice, your sangha is the people who travel with you on your journey to more extraordinary forms of happiness. They help you to stay on your path and become part of who you are. I doubt that extraordinary happiness is possible if it is not shared with others.

Positive psychologists have consistently found that people who are more connected—in committed relationships and nurturing friendships—are happier and healthier. There are many explanations for why this may be the case, but Buddhists offer a unique perspective on the matter. Rather than seeing the self as a separate entity from others, Buddhists see our identities as intimately related. Thich Nhat Hanh, a prominent Vietnamese teacher, uses the term *interbeing* to describe our interconnection with others and all of life, which is our primary identity. Rather than an individual who interacts with distinct others, he sees each of us as integral parts of a larger whole. From this perspective, your happiness is tied to everyone else's. If I go about seeking happiness in a way that prohibits others from seeking their form of happiness, we will ultimately cause each other less happiness. So, with each step on our journey toward happiness, we will be happier when it is shared with and promotes the happiness of others.

UPDATING YOUR MAP: ALWAYS THE SAME OR ALWAYS CHANGING?

Perhaps one of the most surprising places Buddhists and positive psychologists agree is in the area of permanence versus impermanence: They agree that one of the secrets to extraordinary happiness is recognizing that all things are constantly changing; all things are impermanent. I find this surprising because it seems that so much of our lives in modern culture focuses on creating security: the promise that things will not change, or if they do, we will get them back to the way they were as soon as possible. Most of us insure our houses, cars, lives, health, vision, teeth, pets' health, bank accounts, vacations, and businesses. If we fear that this is not enough, we get umbrella insurance to add extra protection. If we could, I am sure most of us would buy insurance to ensure that our marriages endured, our families never became ill, and our jobs were guaranteed for life. Although there is nothing wrong with the basic concept of insurance (I have as much or more than most), I think our absolute fascination with it points to a deeper fear: a fear of our lives changing.

PERMANENCE VERSUS IMPERMANENCE

Positive psychologists have found an interesting difference between pessimists and optimists. Pessimists tend to see *negative* events as permanent and good events as temporary.[3] Optimists have the opposite tendency: They see *good* events as permanent and bad events as temporary. As you might expect, researchers have consistently found that optimists tend to be happier people.

The Buddhists add an interesting twist: They see *both* positive and negative events as temporary. They base this on the assumption that things are always changing: We are born, grow up, grow old, and eventually die. All living things follow the same pattern. Everything humans create— whether physical (pyramids, cars, houses, books) or social (nations, religions, friendships)—has its time of glory but eventually declines, decays, or radically changes to survive in new times. So, Buddhists use a wide-angle lens. When good events come, they celebrate them, knowing all the while that eventually things will change. When difficult times come, they do not become overly distressed or hopeless: They know, this too shall pass.[4] This *wide-angle lens of wisdom* allows them to embrace the circle of life and death with grace and peace. They practice equanimity.[5] It appears to be one of the secrets to extraordinary happiness.

The Three Attitudes

	Bad Events	*Good Events*
Pessimism	**Permanent** "Bad things always happen to me."	**Temporary** "I got lucky this time."
Optimism	**Temporary** "I had a bad day."	**Permanent** "Good things always come my way."
Equanimity	**Temporary** "This is not what I was hoping for; this too shall pass."	**Temporary** "This is what I have been hoping for: I will enjoy it, knowing it too will change."

PESSIMISTIC TO ENLIGHTENED RESPONSES

Exercise: From Pessimistic to Enlightened Responses

Download worksheet at www.mindfulnessforchocolate.com.

Identify two negative and two positive events in your life, either single occurrences or reoccurring events. Write out the old response (believing this is permanent) and revise to a more enlightened response. Remember, both pessimism and optimism involve viewing things as permanent; pessimists believe the negative events are permanent and optimists view the positive as permanent. The Buddhists view it all as temporary.

	Old Response: This is permanent.	**Enlightened Response:** This is temporary.
Example: My best friend is pulling away from me.	*I should have seen this coming OR I wonder why she doesn't like me anymore.*	*This friendship is changing; perhaps it will return to where it was before or perhaps we need something different right now.*
Negative Event No. 1		
Negative Event No. 2		
Positive Event No. 1		
Positive Event No. 2		

GETTING LOST: THE WISDOM OF NOT KNOWING

One of my favorite things to do when I visit the town center of a historic city is to get lost. For example, in Europe, after locating the church or building that marks the heart of the city, I just start walking down any street that looks interesting. Curiosity typically leads me to the smaller, quieter streets to avoid the obvious tourist attractions, and instead I seek to discover the city as the locals—past and present—have done for centuries.

Soon, I find myself enchanted by what is otherwise the "ordinary life" of the inhabitants. Each time I turn a corner I am promised a new experience—an open market with food and crafts, a tiny baroque church sandwiched between modern apartments, a stone staircase so narrow I must slip through sideways, an elderly woman sweeping her porch, or the aroma of lunch being prepared at a small cafe.

On such walks, my mind is totally open—open and willing to see and appreciate whatever is there. I delight in the freedom and excitement of not knowing what lies around the corner. In her brilliantly fun book, *Outrageous Openness*, Tosha Silver describes the art of living with such openness as letting the divine take the lead—or driver's seat—trusting God, universal intelligence, or whatever benevolent force you believe organizes the universe to safely guide you where you need to go.[6]

However, I struggle to live the rest of my life with the same wild openness to the moment. When the "adventure" involves my career, finances, love life, family life, social network, or schedule, I do *not* find joy in "not knowing" what's coming. Instead, I want a plan and people whom I can count on. I want to know what will be there tomorrow; I want to know where I am today; I want to understand what happened yesterday. I want a sense of control over my life. But there is a cost to having this sense of control: the price is a big chunk of your happiness.

LOSING CONTROL

For most of us, the idea of "losing control" is a frightening one. We will do most anything to maintain control of our emotions, our partners, our children, our jobs, our finances, and our schedules. In fact, most psychopathology is rooted in some form of this fear. The hidden assumption is that if we are not in control, then someone else is controlling us. In this paradigm or map of life, one person is in control and the other is not—and we'd all rather be the one in control. The Buddhists see things entirely differently—they have a different map of how things work. When you assume that things are always changing—and recognize how little control we have over external things changing—it is easier to be at peace with losing control and not knowing. You learn the true meaning of the word "yes."

SAYING "YES"

Summed up in one word, Buddhists say "yes" to life—all of life, the good, the bad, the expected, the unexpected. This is not the yes of over-indulgence or resignation, but rather the yes of "I am open to my present moment experience—all of it, regardless of whether it is what I want." Whether things are difficult (such as losing a loved one) or unpredictable (your flight was just canceled halfway to your destination), the default and only answer is "yes" I will walk this path too—and see where it leads.

I can remember one time when I was able to practice this. I was flying to a one-day board meeting in San Diego from Fresno in central California. I was driving a colleague to the airport at 4:30 in the morning and ended up missing the exit because I was more engrossed in our conversation than the destination. We ended up missing our flight and were then booked on another flight that went through San Francisco before connecting to a plane in Los Angeles that would take us to San Diego. At first, I was very frustrated with myself and the lack of alternative possibilities, but then I realized that there was nothing I could do. I surrendered to what I could not change and decided it could be an adventure of sorts since San Francisco is a city that I love. My attitude of adventure served me well; my colleague knew of a great bookstore in the San Francisco airport. In our somewhat extended layover, I found a stack of books that eventually paved the way to a whole new method of teaching my classes and working with clients. If I had stayed in a frantic, woe-is-me state of mind, I think I would have missed this incredible opportunity. We made it to our meeting only thirty minutes late, laughing and humbled by saying "yes" to what seemed at the time such a great misfortune.

YOU NEVER KNOW WHAT LIES AHEAD

Have you ever heard any of your single or divorcing friends say, "But all the good ones are taken"? I always wonder how people come to this conclusion: based on the available singles at their job, an online search, their married life, or reports of their friends? According to governmental statistics, thousands of "good ones" get married every day. And, if the "good ones" are actually choosing to get married, that should give a single person seeking to marry a "good one" hope, not reason for despair—at least, if they are leading a life of extraordinary happiness.

When your life map assumes scarcity rather than abundance, that perspective has a profound effect on your ability to create a life of extraordinary happiness: you cannot get where you want to go because your assumption of scarcity does not even put your destination on the map. I have worked with countless people wanting to be in a committed relationship who insist at twenty, thirty, forty, fifty, and sixty that "all the good ones are taken"—their true goal never even makes it onto their map.

So, it is key to remember that we never get to see the entire map, at least during this lifetime. That is what makes life the adventure that it is. Life is full of surprises—some pleasant, some not—but if you know *how* to travel, the journey is worth overcoming the bumps, dead ends, and bad weather.

Exercise: Getting Lost: Not Knowing and Losing Control

Download worksheet at www.mindfulnessforchocolate.com.

Identify at least one way you can begin to play with "not knowing" and losing control in each area of your life.

	Not Knowing and Losing Control
Example: Personal	*Instead of getting angry the next time I end up in a long line, I wonder if this is a sign that I need to slow down.*
Personal Physical and emotional health; identity; self-esteem	
Relationships Significant other, children, parents, friends, coworkers	
Career/Education Career decisions; attitude toward work	

	Not Knowing and Losing Control
Example: Personal	*Instead of getting angry the next time I end up in a long line, I wonder if this is a sign that I need to slow down.*
Spiritual Spiritual practice; time for reflection, etc.	
Financial/Everyday Stuff Managing finances; daily routine and stressors	

FROM MAP TO MANDALA

Most people find that visual aids facilitate learning, and some just want an excuse to be crafty, while others like an excuse to practice graphic design. If you fall into any of these categories, you may enjoy the following somewhat artsy exercise. If such things have no appeal, feel free to skip ahead. But if you want to try to find an excuse to play, read on.

Tibetan Buddhists use *mandalas* for meditation. Mandalas are literally a form of cosmic map that depicts various Buddhas or other Buddhist teachings. They typically have one primary Buddha in the center surrounded by other Buddhas and other sacred beings based on teachings related to that Buddha. Other mandalas depict sacred teachings, such as the various heavens and hells. Mandalas provide an artistic and visual representation of sacred teachings. Now that you have begun to outline your personal cosmic map, it might be fun to create your personal mandala. You can start by filling in the blank mandala provided on page 46.

Step 1: Choose a Format

Buddhist mandalas most often have a central figure surrounded by four others: north, south, east, and west, forming a cross. If you are of Christian background, you may want to envision this as a cross. If you are of Jewish background, you may want to create a six-pointed mandala to represent the Star of David. If you love chocolate, you might want to organize yours like your favorite box of chocolates.

Step 2: Choose a Center

The center of the mandala should represent the "heart" of your map. By reviewing your answers to the questions above, you should be able to identify the core belief, value, or person that is at the center of your life. You may choose a symbol that represents God, spirit, self, life, peace, love, family, favorite dessert, or whatever emerged as a central theme.

Step 3: Choose Your Sub-Themes

Once you have chosen the heart, then choose a theme or person for each of the major quadrants of your mandala. If you chose to use a cross format, you will need four more; if you chose a Star of David, you would need six more. It is often helpful to pair opposites, such as Self and Relationships; Work and Play; Spirit and Body, or whatever comes to mind based on the answers to your questions earlier in the chapter.

Step 4: Fill It In

Finally, begin writing in words or adding pictures that speak to what each quadrant is about. For the more creative types, you can create your own out of paper or wood and create a collage with photos, magazine clippings, fabrics, symbolic objects, or whatever else seems right.

    The purpose of this exercise is to help you become more aware and mindful of how you view yourself, life, and others. The more conscious you are of where your ideas, opinions, and feelings come from, the easier it is to make changes in areas that are not working for you.

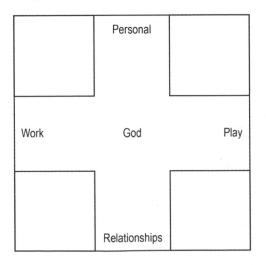

· 4 ·

Who Moved My Chocolate?

Befriending Problems, Befriending Life

$\mathcal{I}$ was seven, and it was the week after Christmas. My room was filled with new toys and games, but one gift was kept hidden. I hid it every year. My father emigrated from Vienna in his early twenties, but his family remained in Europe. Each Christmas the last gift opened was the box from Vienna, always filled with unimaginable delights that my American eyes had never seen: replicas of royal trinkets, an embroidered coin purse, hand-knit sweaters, dolls in traditional dress, and always the *best* chocolate. My father would dutifully divide the treats equally among the three kids, my mother bequeathing her share to us. Before I went to bed, I made sure the chocolate was well hidden so that my siblings wouldn't "accidentally" confuse mine with theirs. Well trained by my mother, whose Greek immigrant parents lost everything in the 1929 crash, I saved my chocolate for the proverbial "rainy day." I decided my underwear drawer would be the one place my siblings would not dare go.

The rain came the following week, so I thought it was time for a small taste from my special stash. I went to my drawer only to find my chocolate was gone. Certain my sister or brother stole it, I confronted them: Who ate it? Total denial. So, I ran to my parents, but what could they do? So, I got angry; I cried, pouted, begged, and screamed. I tore my room apart in hopes that I had hidden it elsewhere and forgotten. Even my dad's willingness to share his stash with me did not ease my pain. I wanted what I wanted, and I wanted it now. No substitutions. I wanted everything to go the way I planned, the way I did it every year. But I couldn't make it so; my parents couldn't either.

Little did I realize at that time, but this scenario would be essentially the same setup for more complicated life problems as I got older. The pattern is this: I want something I think I should have but I do not get it for whatever reason, sometimes without ever having a good explanation as to why not or what "really" happened. I have learned that I can continue to throw tantrums each time life does not go my way—hopefully in a more sophisticated way than I did as a child—or I can find a new way to relate to problems and the many faces of suffering I inevitably continue to encounter in my life. In my quest, I have discovered that the Buddhists have an antidote for such tantrums that they sum up in their foundational truths.

BUDDHIST VIEW OF PROBLEMS: THE FOUR NOBLE TRUTHS

The Buddhists have Four Noble Truths that are helpful when problems are as small as someone stealing your chocolate or as dramatic as losing the love of your life.[1] These truths describe how Buddhists view suffering and their approach to skillfully coping with it.

The First Noble Truth is that there is suffering in life. Most of us hear this, shut the book, and walk away. But if you read further, the Buddha offered insight and hope on the matter. He explained that while some forms of suffering are inevitable—illness, change, and death—most of our suffering is of our own making. This is not a particularly cheery idea until you realize that this means we have viable options for reducing most of the suffering in our lives.

This brings us to the Second Noble Truth, which identifies the underlying source of suffering. The Buddha taught that our suffering is primarily caused by our *attachments*, our ideas about how life "should" go. The more strongly attached we are to a person, idea, or thing, the more we suffer in relation to it. For example, while writing this sentence, I am hoping it will be helpful to you, the reader, and approved of by my publisher. That hope is a form of attachment. If I am strongly attached, I will feel hurt or angry if anybody criticizes a single sentence. If I am less attached, I will hear feedback as valuable information about how to improve and will be able to acknowledge that the proper place for this sentence may actually be in my computer's trashcan. To trip us up even more, our attachments are generally double sided: We strongly want things to go one way and definitely do not want things to go the opposite way, resulting in a cascade of disappointments. In all cases, the stronger our attachment, the greater we suffer in relation to it.

The Third Noble Truth is that the cessation of suffering can be achieved by cultivating non-attachment. Third time is always a charm. In fact, I think the Buddha should have started here. Suffering can end—or at least be greatly reduced. Even though suffering is inherent to living, a person can learn ways to greatly reduce, and for those enlightened few, actually eliminate it. Most of us do not fall into the latter, but all of us can certainly take small steps to actually reduce how much we suffer. The most exciting part is that rather than reduce suffering incident by incident, there are ways to lower suffering across the board by cultivating certain habits.

Finally, the Fourth Noble Truth, the Eightfold Path, describes how a person can go about reducing attachment. The Eightfold Path is divided into three areas: mental concentration (chapter 5), wisdom (chapters 6 and 7), and ethics (chapter 8). The last two areas are familiar to most of us because they have parallels in the Judeo-Christian tradition. But historically mental concentration has been rarely discussed or practiced in the Western world. Thus, Buddhism provides Westerners with a new tool for reducing suffering in our lives, which may explain why mental concentration practices such as mindfulness have become so popular in recent years. Together, these three components of the Eightfold Path are designed to do one thing: reduce the root source of suffering—our attachments.

ATTACHMENT AND SUFFERING

Why are attachments such a problem? After all, isn't it only "natural" to have preferences, hopes, and desires? If I let go of these, how could I be happy and who would I be? How could letting go of these possibly lead to *extraordinary* happiness? These questions come to mind for most of us when we first hear about the Buddhist idea of attachment. First, I think it is important to understand that the Buddhists use the term "attachment" differently than modern psychologists, who use it to refer to the healthy, positive emotional bond between child and caregiver or two lovers. In contrast, Buddhists use the term to refer to a negative reactive attachment to an idea, person, or thing and dependence on that object for one's happiness.[2] As someone whose professional life requires discussing both forms of attachment, I would have recommended the Buddhist term to be translated as "clinging" or "grasping," which it sometimes is in classic Eastern text translations. If you have a background in psychology and dual use of the term is torturous, feel free to use one of these alternatives. Alternatively, you may want to use the closest correlate in Western psychology to the Buddhist idea of attachment, which is the concept of internal and external locus of control.

ATTACHMENT: EXTERNAL VERSUS INTERNAL LOCUS OF CONTROL

I have seen it many times. A client is miraculously cured of depression. The antidote is not Prozac, Zoloft, or any other miracle drug. It is not the brilliant session we had the week prior. No, nothing like that at all. She fell in love; his estranged wife returned; he got the job he'd been dreaming of; she finally got pregnant. They feel great—on top of the world—and often do not feel that they need to continue with therapy. The insurance companies would agree: no depressive symptoms this week, why should we pay? But let's pause to consider what really happened. The outside world changed to fulfill their hopes, and so their mood changed. So what is the problem? On one level it is great: pull out the champagne (except if you are pregnant), get some flowers, and grab a box of chocolate—and celebrate. I am all for it—especially the chocolate part. The problem arises when this is a person's *only* or primary method for achieving happiness. With this approach, the outside world must continue to conform to their wishes for them to be happy. I have yet to find someone who knows how to make life compliant to his or her every wish. Eventually, life happens: something or someone changes, and happiness evaporates. The roller coaster continues (that's when I, the therapist, get the call that the client needs to see me again). This is why in the search for greater happiness we need to examine what psychologists call "locus of control."

Locus of control is a fundamental concept in cognitive psychology.[3] People who have an external locus of control view the external world as the primary source of control of their lives and destinies. Such people frequently say "You made me feel . . ."; "It is so unfair"; "If only X didn't happen or Y didn't do so and so, I'd be happy, feel better, or would have done a better job." In sum, they blame something outside themselves when life does not go their way. They often feel like victims and can be quite angry or hopeless about it. They feel victimized because the primary lens through which they see life has an arrow going one way—the outside world is targeting them. Anything from bad moods to bad weather is viewed as the outside world doing something *to* me: my spouse was insensitive *to me*, my kids were not listening *to me*, or the bad weather spoiled *my plans* (grammarians, notice the use of passive voice and objects).

External locus of control can also take a subtler form: people pleasing. Although arguably the most pleasant people on the planet, people pleasers need the external world to validate their feelings and worth. Without the outside world's approval, they start to crumble. They get angry, feel worthless, or become depressed. This type of person *does* tend to make others and themselves happy for a time, but their personal happiness is left in a precarious position: it requires that others continually show appreciation and agreement with their efforts. This method inevitably fails to sustain their and others' happiness, resulting in divorce, depression, affairs, anxiety, mid-life crises, and other life-altering events that keep therapists like myself employed. Good therapists cure them of being overly generous; ineffective ones stay employed for years.

In contrast, psychologists describe internal locus of control as a person's sense of self and worth coming from within. When things go wrong, they do not blame others but instead check to see what they might have done to cause this and always focus on what useful actions they can take to respond to the current situation (grammarians, notice the active voice). They rarely have a sense of hopelessness because they see themselves as active agents in their lives rather than victims. They set realistic goals and achieve them, regardless of the challenges that arise. When they are victims of violent crime or social injustice, they feel fear, anger, hurt, and even doubt themselves, humanity, and God. They experience the trauma and find meaningful ways to work through it, no matter how long it takes or how hard it is. In the end, they are resilient, bouncing back by finding a way to use the injustice to create something good even from the most horrific of life experiences. They never allow their abusers the ultimate win by remaining a psychological victim. For me, Viktor Frankl provides the paramount example of this: After surviving the horrors of Nazi prison camps, he used these experiences to develop a psychological approach that teaches how to find meaning from such experiences.[4]

The Buddhist aim to cultivate non-attachment has many parallels with internal versus external locus of control. When you are "attached" to an idea, person, or thing, the object of your attachment determines your happiness. If it is an idea, you need to have it validated, adhered to, and enacted to be happy. If it is a person, you need that person to behave and interact in specific ways for you to feel joy. If it is a thing, you need to possess or have access to it in some way to feel fulfilled. In contrast, a person with a greater sense of internal locus of control may have preferences—even strong preferences—for certain ideas, people, and things, but they are able to be happy whether or not the external world unfolds as they desire. They may be disappointed, sad, or even angry when things do not go according to their preferences, but this emotional response is mild and short-lived. It does not disrupt their underlying sense of peace and joy.

EXERCISE: LOCUS OF CONTROL QUIZ

Download worksheet at www.mindfulnessforchocolate.com.

T = mostly true for you; F = mostly false for you.

____ T ____ F   1. I feel that I earn the respect and recognition I deserve.
____ T ____ F   2. Without deadlines and negative consequences, I don't usually finish on time.
____ T ____ F   3. I often worry about what others think of me and my work.
____ T ____ F   4. I like a challenge.
____ T ____ F   5. Most of my success can be attributed to good luck.
____ T ____ F   6. I am confident that I will be OK in the end.
____ T ____ F   7. I need to be in control of a situation to feel OK.
____ T ____ F   8. If a person doesn't like me, it is hard for me to work with that person.
____ T ____ F   9. I usually succeed at my goals.
____ T ____ F   10. I've noticed that hard work always pays off.

Scoring

Tally how many Ts you have for 1, 4, 6, 9, 10: ____/5.
Tally how many Fs you have for 2, 3, 5, 7, 8: ____/5.
Total points: ____/10.
The greater your score, the greater your sense of internal locus of control.

NON-ATTACHMENT: EMBRACING LIFE

As can be reasonably assumed, if we are striving to not be attached, we are working toward non-attachment. Non-attachment is not detachment or a state in which a person is too "enlightened" to have a negative thought or emotion, although I have met some people who seem to have this interpretation. Instead, non-attachment is a counterintuitive approach to problems, an approach that makes us *more* alive to life rather than detached from it. Our natural, hard-wired instinct is to recoil from problems; this is our stress response or fight-flight-freeze mechanism at work. When danger is perceived, we are wired to escape it by fighting it, running from it, or trying to hide from it. But that does not lead to greater peace, joy, and happiness unless it is a saber-toothed tiger that is trying to eat you for lunch. In which case, please—fight, run, or hide.

Instead, non-attachment, much like internal locus of control, does not mean that we perceive the outside world or negative events as the enemy of our happiness. Rather, the external world and its happenings are just *what is*. Non-attachment is simply recognizing and keeping our hearts open to *what is* despite what we might prefer. Although accepting that we are not getting what we want is not easy, when we can do so, the suffering is paradoxically diminished. Similar to entering a cold pool or removing a Band-Aid, the overall level of suffering is generally reduced by willingly and knowingly engaging the discomfort. Please note that if these metaphors do not work for you, the Buddhist teachings still hold true. I happen to prefer slowly entering a cold pool and choose to accept the prolonged suffering, but I prefer to rip off Band-Aids. My kids jump in the pool, but they would prefer their Band-Aids decay before I am allowed to remove them (but when they slumber, the Band-Aid fairy visits).

In my practice as a psychotherapist, much of the suffering I see directly results from a person's attempt to not acknowledge or feel *what is*, because it is too painful, frightening, or overwhelming. In frantic attempts to avoid *what is*, people engage in behaviors such as depression, anxiety, eating disorders, substance abuse, psychosis, and violence, unintentionally creating greater and greater forms of suffering. Ultimately, my job is to bring them back to face the original "overwhelming" truth, which they must now face in the aftermath of the avoidance tactics.

Buddhists and Western psychologists describe similar roads to happiness. Non-attachment and internal locus of control do similar things: they help us to see that whether or not a situation makes us "feel happy" is entirely up to us. For Buddhists, spiritual growth includes learning to not blindly give in to the natural human tendency to be fearfully attached. Thus Buddhist practices focus on reducing the practitioner's attachment to lessen a person's overall level of suffering. One of my favorite exercises for examining attachment is Chocolate Meditation No. 2. This second chocolate meditation extends the principles of the chocolate meditation in chapter 1 to explore the rich complexity of attachment in more depth.

CHOCOLATE MEDITATION NO. 2: EMBRACING WHITE, MILK, AND DARK

You can access the guided meditation at www.mindfulnessforchocolatelovers.com or use this meditation guide and follow along.

Materials

For this exercise, you need to have on hand three forms of chocolate, such as milk, white, and dark (or substitute three forms of any similar type of food, such as nuts, fruits, etc.). All should be unwrapped.

- One must be a form of chocolate (or other food) you feel neutral about.
- One must be a form of chocolate (or other food) you love to eat—preferably your favorite.
- One must be a form of chocolate (or other food) you dislike—yes, you read correctly—something you avoid eating at all costs.

Setup

Begin by placing the three objects in front of you in a row, beginning with the "neutral" object, then "most preferred," and lastly the "least preferred." As we move through this exercise, I want you to begin by pretending you have never experienced any of these objects. Sometimes it helps to think of yourself as an anthropologist studying a long-lost ancient site, such as a Mayan temple to the chocolate gods. Try to get your mind into an open and curious state.

Neutral Chocolate/Food

Pick up the neutral object with your nondominant hand and notice the following:

- *Color:* Notice the shades of color and how the light reflects off the object.
- *Shapes:* Notice the shape and any markings. If there are letters, notice the shapes of the letters and avoid thinking about the words they may form; simply notice the shapes and contours, and do your best to experience the letters without connecting them to conventional meaning.
- *Texture:* Next, notice the texture: Is it smooth, rough, hard, soft?
- *Scent:* Bring it toward your nose and observe the qualities of the scent of the object: Is it pungent, sweet, floral, spicy, fruity, strong, light?
- *Notice Your Thoughts and Feelings:* Bring the object up to your mouth as if you were going to eat it, but **do not** do so. Notice if your body reacts at all. Do you start to salivate? Notice the thoughts and feelings going through your mind: Is there a sense of anticipation or frustration? Just notice how your body and mind respond, trying not to judge what is going on as good or bad. Just curiously observe what your body is doing.
- *One Bite:* Take a bite, allowing the object to sit on your tongue rather than chewing it. Notice its texture: smooth, hard, porous, soft. Is it cold, warm, hot? Notice the taste: Is it sweet, salty, bitter, sour? Roll it around your tongue and notice if it tastes different on different parts of your tongue. *Try not to evaluate whether you like the taste.* Just notice how it tastes. Notice how your body may be responding: Does it begin to crave more? Does it want to stop eating? Does your breathing or heart rate change? Notice without judging or reacting. Go ahead and finish mindfully eating this object.

Preferred Chocolate/Food

Pick up the preferred chocolate with your nondominant hand and mindfully observe and then taste using the same steps as the first object.

Least Preferred Chocolate/Food

Finally, pick up the least preferred chocolate with your nondominant hand and mindfully observe and then taste using the same steps as the first object.

Questions for Reflection

- Did you notice anything you had never noticed previously about the objects?
- Even if your ranking of favorites is the same, has your view of any of them shifted in any way?
- Do you have any new insight into how you form preferences, opinions, and attachments?

I find that everyone has a different experience doing this exercise—and that is the point: for each person to examine the truth of their own experience. Unlike Judeo-Christian religions, Buddhism is not based on faith. From the Buddha to the Dalai Lama, Buddhists teachers don't try to convince you of anything. Instead, they recommend research and consistently say with non-attachment in their voice: "Don't take my word for it. Try it, and see what happens." In this same spirit, I would like to share my personal experience with this meditation.

What I enjoy most about this exercise—besides an educational excuse to eat chocolate—is becoming aware of how arbitrary and flimsy my attachments are. I am often shocked and, quite frankly, humbled to realize how similar the experience of mindfully eating each is. In essence, they all offer rich and full aromatic, visual, flavor, and tactile experiences, especially if I can quiet my mind's desire to label each experience as preferred or not. Nonetheless, once the meditation is over, what I tell myself about each is different, and in fact, my identity is, in a small way, tied to my preferences.

I am actually quite picky about my chocolate: I like moderately dark chocolate, 60 to 80 percent cocoa—a wimp in the minds of those who are eating dark chocolate that is 80+ percent cocoa (you probably have better genetics than the rest of us). And, if we want to be exact, the chocolate I like needs to be really pure—fewer than six ingredients—and have whole hazelnuts to really hit the spot. Even after doing this exercise many times, my preference in everyday life has not changed. Instead, my *relationship to my preference* has changed: I no longer believe my preference has any significant meaning or is in any way better or worse than any other preference. However, in the past, I had more of an opinion that I sometimes took seriously. I would arrogantly say that white chocolate *isn't* chocolate at all and that milk chocolate was made for kids. Ironically, after having children, I am quick to sell them on the idea that white chocolate (which contains only trace caffeine from the cocoa butter) *is* chocolate and insist on the milkiest, least caffeinated chocolate I can find for them (because even though I love them more than life itself, their bedtime is my sane-time).

Somehow, over the years, I have become freer in relationship to this preference. I can see and laugh at its arbitrariness while I still turn down most forms of chocolate that do not fit within my parameters. However, I do so primarily for the benefit of my waistline. Thus, I have the same preference and similar behaviors, but an entirely different relationship to my preference. The real change is the freedom that comes from knowing that my preference is arbitrary, illusory, and self-created; this keeps me laughing at myself and more open to others and life. In fact, this exercise makes me eager to better understand people who have a passion for some other form of chocolate. Transferring this insight to difficult topics, such as a breakup, rejection, or criticism, is a more difficult task but is essentially the same process. The wisdom I have gained from Chocolate Meditation No. 2 allows me to be more open to other realities and possibilities in these situations. In short, this is the art and heart of befriending problems.

BEFRIENDING PROBLEMS:
MAKING FRIENDS WITH WHAT IS

> *Feelings like disappointment, embarrassment, irritation, resentment, anger, jealousy, and fear, instead of being bad news, are actually very clear moments that teach us where it is that we're holding back. . . . They're like messengers that show us, with terrifying clarity, exactly where we're stuck.*[5]
>
> —Pema Chödrön

The wisdom of non-attachment is most applicable when dealing with life's problems: whether small irritants or major life losses. The secret is to befriend our problems and create new relationships with them. This does not imply that Buddhists are masochists who seek out problems and suffering or that they choose to deeply feel and get lost in negative emotions like anger, hate, or irritation. Instead, they invite problems to *play*.

A playful and friendly attitude toward problems begins by being curious and open to learning about their role in your life. Think of yourself a year ago at this time. Can you remember what you were really worried about? How much of that is worth worrying about today? Think of what you were worried about five years ago. How much of that is worth worrying about now? Think of what you were worrying about yesterday. How much of that is meaningful today? For most of us, the answers to these questions reveal that we remember very little about the things we agonized over in the past and that the things we worry about are rarely of consequence. I find this a helpful place to begin because most of the problems that consume our mind throughout the day—Are we going to be late? What should we have for dinner? I disagree with my boss's idea! My spouse was short with me this morning!—these are transient and do not visit for long. They are not as scary, big, or important as they feel in the moment, making them excellent candidates for learning the art of befriending problems.

So, what does this look like in real life? Let's take an ordinary example. Perhaps you have a parent who tends to share less-than-useful or perhaps even hurtful comments each time you speak. Your typical reaction may be to get annoyed, shoot back some hurtful comments, and/or quietly sulk. Befriending the problem in this situation would require looking at the comments that irritate you and developing a new relationship to them. In my case, my father is a storyteller, which is great except for the fact that he tends to tell the same story over and over again, reiterating the same life lessons I have heard for decades. Rather than roll my eyes or debate the point, I have learned to listen and play a little game: I ask myself what part he has added, stretched, or left out in this particular telling of the story. Has he changed the story based on the audience or current event? Does he actually have a point this time? By viewing the situation in a new light, I develop a playful and even appreciative attitude toward the same behavior—and we are both much happier in the end. Sometimes I laugh at the end of a story I have heard one hundred times; other times I laugh because he, like all of us, has his colorful and unending quirks. Sometimes the best response is just to delight in the zaniness of it all.

FIVE STEPS TO BEFRIENDING PROBLEMS

The seeds of wisdom, peace, and wholeness are within each of our difficulties.[6]

—Jack Kornfield

How do you befriend problems? On one level it is quite simple: It is a *choice*. Each time you identify something as a problem in your life, you choose to see it as a friend, perhaps a messenger, or simply another opportunity to do something different. The problem is, most of us are so conditioned to mindlessly react to problems that the alternative to "do something different" requires discipline. However—ultimately—this is the only actual challenge. I have learned from my work as a therapist, once you can calm your emotional reactivity, most of us are quite capable of creatively, meaningfully, and playfully coping with life stressors. The hardest part is interrupting our reactivity cycle. To help interrupt this cycle, I recommend these five steps:

1. **Identify the Problem:** What exactly is the problem and why is it a problem for *you?*
2. **Identify Its Effects:** Identify the negative and positive effects of the problem in all aspects of your life.
3. **Identify Your Reaction:** Identify how you react to the problem and the effects of your reaction on your life.
4. **Identify Potentials for Friendship:** Identify avenues for befriending problems.
5. **Identify Small Action Steps:** Identify small, realistic steps for action.

STEP 1: IDENTIFY THE PROBLEM

It's strange. When we have a problem, it seems painfully clear to us that it is a problem. But when asked *how* or *in what way* it is a problem, it is hard for most of us to articulate. Too often, the bottom line is this: "I am not getting what I want." It is that simple. For example, if the airport security line is taking too long, I may miss my flight or, even worse, not have enough time to change my child's diaper before getting on the plane, which of course might cause a person to not get what they want: to sit back, relax, and enjoy the flight. Similarly, when I go to a restaurant and do not enjoy the meal or find the wait staff unhelpful, I could let this ruin the evening. But, again, I simply am not getting what I want or what I think I should have. When I get into a disagreement with a colleague, a friend, or my partner, I could be upset because the other person is not agreeing with me; I could even take it personally or as a sign that there is something wrong with the other person or our relationship. Yet, this is also another instance in which I am essentially not getting what I want on at least two levels: I am not having an easy conversation with this person, and the outcome of our discussion may also threaten something else that I want.

Most often, when I ask myself, "What's the bottom-line problem here?" it becomes clear that this is what I call a "milk-white-or-dark" issue: It is a matter of preference. The question then becomes, How important is this preference for me? Is it worth fighting for? If there are multiple preferences at stake, which is most important to me? How do I focus on this priority? Sometimes this first step is all it takes to shrink a big headache into a good-sized laugh.

STEP 2: IDENTIFYING NEGATIVE AND POSITIVE EFFECTS

The next step is to identify the negative and positive effects of the problem. I think it is helpful to explore how the problem affects your life in all areas: physical, emotional, spiritual, relational, occupational, and social. We generally view a problem as affecting one area of our life; however, most problems trickle over into other areas. For example, if you are not happy with your weight (physical), you may find it spills over to your self-confidence in your relationships (social), your job (work), and even your relationship to God (spiritual). Similarly, you may also find that there are surprising positive effects. Perhaps you have joined a gym (physical) with your partner (relational) and met a new friend (social) or a new business contact (work) while working out. Even with the worst life events—death of a loved one, divorce, life-threatening illness, or sexual abuse—there ultimately is some sort of potential positive developments if you can compassionately stay with them.

In fact, the bigger the problem, the greater the possibility of positive effects in the long run. For example, I have worked with hundreds of people who were abused as children; of course, the immediate effects of the abuse were horrific. However, the typically arduous and long healing process often brings with it unexpected strengths, freedom, friendships, spirituality, and self-respect, which many say that they would have never found without the journey of healing. This does *not* mean that abuse is not a real problem and that we should stop worrying about it happening to children. I believe it is one of the most significant problems our society has yet to seriously address; however, I also know the healing journey can bring with it unique gifts that can shape a person's life in positive ways to help counterbalance the abuse itself.

STEP 3: IDENTIFYING YOUR REACTION

The next step is to examine how you react to the problem. When faced with the same problem, we all react differently. So, what are your favorite ways to react: Do you become angry, fearful, or irritated? Do you obsess over it, ignore it, hide it, or dwell on it? Do you feel cheated, freeze up, or gear up for action? Do you become hopeless, highly emotional, or overly logical? Do you react the same to all problems? When do you do what?

Once you identify your reaction, the next question is: How does this affect the situation? In what ways does your response make things better? In what ways worse? Although we dislike answering these questions, the answers offer insight into how we habitually relate to problems, and often those insights are enough to inspire us to do something different. Typically, when we analyze our reaction to problems, we find we go to war with problems, try to evict them from our lives as quickly as possible, or pretend they are not there. This is where befriending problems can offer a fresh way to respond.

STEP 4: IDENTIFY POTENTIALS FOR FRIENDSHIP

Rather than ignore or attack the problem, take a moment to relate to it a bit differently. Some options include:

- **Curiosity:** Often it helps to be curious about it. What do you not know about the problem or situation? What other reasonable explanations could there be for the situation? Perhaps you made assumptions about another's intentions or the actual possibilities in a situation? Sometimes when we soften by becoming curious about what is going on, we discover answers and possibilities we could not see in our reactive and panicked state.
- **Problem as Teacher:** For many, it is helpful to wonder about possible lessons you are being allowed to learn. What are you

being asked to learn about life, yourself, your relationship, or the human condition by this problem situation?

- **Problem as Preparation:** In what ways might the problem be preparation for things to come? Might it be an opportunity to face a long-held fear? Is there a possible purpose for the problem that we cannot yet see?

- **Just Is What Is:** Other times, it is helpful to acknowledge that this is just how things are in life, at least at this moment. Open-heartedly accepting what is must be distinguished from hopeless resignation. Embracing what is—in the Buddhist tradition—results in a sense of freedom and liberation.

- **Situation without Your Interpretation:** If you could be in this exact situation without the ability to think that it was a problem—that the situation just "was," as natural as wind and rain, how would you respond differently? What thoughts and actions might be different?

Each situation must be befriended on its own terms. For example, traffic or a delayed train can be viewed as a divine permission for quiet, peaceful time in an otherwise hectic schedule; a bad restaurant meal, a nice compliment on your own or spouse's home cooking; an argument with a friend, an opportunity to deepen the connection by moving beyond Pollyanna conversation. In most cases, if you can come up with even one *plausible* alternative, your stress level goes down and you can find a more proactive and effective way to approach the situation.

STEP 5: IDENTIFY SMALL STEPS

The most important step is to do something—even a little something—*different*. Notice, I said different, not better or more correct. I recommend that you come up with small, realistic steps for action based on what has worked for you in the past. For example, if you choose to view being stuck in traffic as a divine permission for some "me" time, prepare yourself by having a special playlist on hand just for this purpose and do not play it unless you are in traffic; promise to stop it when traffic clears up. During a lousy meal out, start planning your next dinner party menu to include a wild reshuffling of the ingredients in the current meal; consider who might need an invitation—perhaps tonight's chef? Use an argument with a friend as an invitation to celebrate the increasing honesty in the relationship: what small gift or act might symbolize this? As you become more comfortable and adventurous with befriending problems, you will be surprised at how quickly things transform and how easily problems can become your best friend.

EXERCISE: BEFRIENDING PROBLEMS WORKSHEET

Download worksheet at www.mindfulnessforchocolate.com.

Choose one problem you are currently struggling with and use this worksheet to help you develop a new way to interact with it.

Step 1: Identify the Problem

Identify the problem in neutral, behavioral terms (describe what a video camera would record in terms of action and words without value-based interpretations such as "rude," "mean," "thoughtless," etc.):

Step 2: Identify Its Effects

Negative Effects: What are the specific effects of the problem in each area of your life?

Physical:

Emotional:

Spiritual:

Relational:

Occupational:

Other:

Positive Effects: Now identify the positive effects: This may take a little more thinking and time. For example, if you are single and want to be in a relationship, is this prompting you to take good care of your body and excel at work? If you are having problems with your spouse, is this prompting you to seek out spiritual guidance or connection with friends and family?

Physical:

Emotional:

Spiritual:

Relational:

Occupational:

Other:

Step 3: Identify Your Reaction

How do you typically react to this problem? Anger, fear, irritation, ignore it, hide it, dwell on it, become hopeless, feel cheated, emotional, logical, increased action, decreased action. List all the responses you can think of:

How do these reactions affect your life?

Negative Effects:

Positive Effects:

Step 4: Identify Potentials for Friendship

Problem as Teacher: Imagine this problem was put into your life to teach you something. What might that be? _____

Problem as Preparation: Imagine this problem or person was sent into your life to prepare you for something. What might that be? _____

Just Is What Is: Imagine this problem "just is" in your life without a specific purpose. What adjustments are you being asked to make? _____

Situation without Your Interpretation: If you were in this exact situation but could not think of it as a problem, how would your thoughts, emotions, and actions be different? _____

Friendship in Action: If you decided to befriend your problem, how might you *behave, relate, and/or feel* differently? _____

Step 5: Small Steps

Identify three small steps you are willing to take toward befriending this problem:

1.

2.

3.

ADVANCED COURSE IN BEFRIENDING PROBLEMS

> *There is no such thing as a problem—just opportunities to learn things that I have not yet mastered.*
>
> —From me to me on a bad day

Once you master the five steps to befriending problems, you may want to advance to this shortcut of an insight: There is no such thing as a problem—just learning opportunities. Going back to your map of the cosmos, if you prefer a more "neutral" view of the cosmos, each perceived "problem" is actually a flashing neon sign pointing to how you need to adjust your map in order for it to more accurately reflect what is. If you prefer a more benevolent view of the universe, a "problem" is a lesson or task that was specifically crafted for you to learn something—problems are oddly disguised gifts, even during the most difficult moments of our lives.

BEFRIENDING THE IMPOSSIBLE

Befriending problems is not so difficult when it involves the little things: long lines, self-doubt, or our partner's foibles. But when the big things hit—a loved one dies, we receive a serious diagnosis, our partner leaves, we lose a job—it becomes much harder to be open, playful, present, or friendly. However, these are the moments most critical to befriend. The costs of not befriending are too high. Yet mustering the courage to open our hearts in these situations sometimes seems too much to bear.

It may take months or even years to get to the point where you can befriend the darkest moments in your life. When tragedy strikes—a loved one is senselessly murdered, your child receives a life-threatening diagnosis, your partner walks out on you and your children, or you contemplate ending your own life—do not rush yourself (and certainly not others) to befriend such moments until you are ready. Sometimes, a long period of profound grieving is necessary before entertaining such an idea. At other times, you may ache so deeply and are so exhausted from grief that you are brought to your knees and are willing to consider that God may not be evil after all and consider another perspective. The one thing I can promise you is that after you do it once, each time thereafter it gets easier.

My first meaningful experience with befriending grief was when my brown-eyed husky died. For those who don't get sentimental about pets, I hope you can indulge the story and perhaps can glean some useful information nonetheless. I got Tara as a puppy five years earlier, shortly after I moved alone to a new town in central California for my first position out of graduate school. She and her sister, a white German Shepherd, were my little family; we had our daily routines, growing pains, and adventures up and down the California coast. Whereas the shepherd appointed herself my loyal protector, Tara took on the roles of family comedian and "princess": she could feel a pea or pebble under the deepest pile of bedding. She kept us laughing all day with wacky doggie habits yet always insisted on a well-made bed with fluffy pillows at bedtime.

However, after the stress of moving to a smaller house in southern California when I got a promotion, she developed an autoimmune disease. I learned to track the severity of her illness by the slightest changes in her behavior or look in her eyes. Despite weakness from the illness, she maintained her playful and mischievous personality and she continued to be an eager running companion. Her joy on the running trail was palpable: every fiber of her being was vibrant and alive. Each time I ran with her, I vowed I would learn to love life as purely and simply as she did, even when I was not well.

After doing well for a while, she took a turn for the worse and was suddenly so weak she could not walk. This time she went to a specialized pet hospital (this is where some of you are rolling your eyes at us pet lovers—understood, especially after I got the bill). During the consultation, the vets were confident that a new diet—perhaps a new protein like kangaroo—would help. I winced, trying to swallow the idea that such protein was legal, but then left hopeful that we were going to have a breakthrough in this yearlong disease. Forty-five minutes later, I got the call. It was cancer—lymphoma of the bowel. I agreed to give her one shot of chemo to see how she responded. When I returned the next morning, the vets, who had been hopeful the day before, told me I should have her put down: there was no response to the chemo.

I was shaking due to the dramatic change in prognosis. Earlier that same year I had watched my aunt, who was a second mother to me, die a horrific death from breast cancer that spread to the lungs, brain, and eventually her whole body (and if you are wondering, no, I did not befriend that loss for a long time). Now Tara faced essentially the same thing, but I was not ready. So, I took her home and set up my own doggie hospice.

Having lost thirteen classmates in high school and college (they have changed California teen driving laws since) and three close family members already, I knew what I had to do. Unlike the friends and family that I had lost before, this loss had an added layer of guilt: Did I do something to cause this, or fail to do something that could have prevented it? At first, I did not believe this was a problem I could befriend. However, at that point in my life, I knew enough about healing the heart and soul that ultimately I had to find a way. I sent my friends and family home to just be with her without distractions. I looked in her eyes and gathered the courage to say, "I will befriend this moment for the two of us. I will keep my heart open in your last hours." As she was my doggie princess, I decided to have a classy little party to celebrate her life—just me, her, and her sisters: the Shepherd and our cat. I turned on James Taylor; it was a night for "Fire and Rain." I pulled out my Viennese crystal and china, the finest Belgian chocolate, and French champagne to toast each precious memory. I cried. I laughed. I sang. I prayed. The Shepherd and cat kept vigil with me, encircling Tara. They knew what was happening, and I was struck by how their natural response was simply to sit and witness Tara's passing. Their perfect stillness and intense focus on their companion created a palpable atmosphere of the sacred, which I have rarely experienced in humans: our minds use language, stories, and our imagination to find infinite ways to escape being present with what is, especially when it is death. We sat and slept next to her well-made princess bed the entire night.

My heart broke that night. But rather than finding it in pieces in the morning, I found it broken wide open—open enough to befriend the death of my beloved companion. The night before, I felt the fullness of my love for her, and I could no longer tell if the tears that fell were tears of joy or sorrow—in fact, they were neither—they were tears of pure love. In the end, I think she taught me the secret of the joy that radiated so freely from her on the trail.

Eventually, we all encounter one of our worst fears—something we believe we cannot bear. It will come, and in fact, such moments typically come several times in all of our lives. In these moments, we will break. Every time. But we must choose whether we break down or *break open*. We will most likely cry, get angry, and feel overwhelmed at first. But at any point, we are free to choose to befriend the moment. The first step is simple but terrifying: acknowledging what has just happened. You may not be able to do this with your first major life tragedy, and that is OK. I could not. But as you practice on the little things, you develop the courage to one day use it with one of your bigger challenges. Each time you do this, you become braver and more confident that you can survive the next round. And, forgive my honesty, but there will be another one most likely at some point—until the day comes when you simply know that no matter what happens, you will not just survive, but grow through it.

In the years since, I discovered that Tara's passing was a gentle warmup exercise for more challenging problems that need befriending: facing unimaginable tragedies, injustice and failures. Each time, my mind initially tries to find some sort of simple explanation or magical solution that will make it all go away. After a couple of failed attempts to use reason to solve the problem, I realize that I need to befriend the nightmarish reality before me. And with each new trial I face, I have learned that if I quiet the part of me that wants to run away from the painful reality, the answer comes—with laser-like clarity and a deep-seated calm in my darkest hour. A voice that I know only from the quietest moments of meditation provides the answer. And if you want to know the truth about meditation, although it is quite useful for daily stresses (you will learn about this in chapter 5), you won't discover the real value of such an arguably boring practice until you face such a moment. When you can still your mind, you can make agonizing decisions with lucidity and peace. You finally know freedom when you can consciously befriend your worst nightmare. Befriending allows you to be fully present when making life-altering decisions that you can then unwaveringly uphold, even in the most unimaginable of circumstances.

Perhaps the most remarkable lesson the Buddhists offer is that simply "being with" a problem radically transforms our experience of it. I encourage you to try this in the Befriending Meditation below.

BEFRIENDING MEDITATION

The Befriending Meditation is grounded in Tibetan Buddhist practices (*Vajrayana*) that use everyday life—the "positive" and the "negative"—to inspire meditation. This particular exercise is derived from the practice of meditation on "wrathful deities," which here symbolize the difficult and dark side of life. I also incorporate elements of Internal Family Systems therapy, an approach often used with survivors of sexual abuse.[7] You can use the guided version on www.mindfulnessfor chocolatelovers.com or use the meditation guide here.

Meditation Preparation

Identify a problem you are having right now, such as arguing with your partner, a professional rejection, missing your lover, struggling with your child's behavior, or being angry at a friend. Choose one problem to focus on. Now, I want you to find something that symbolizes the issue with which you are struggling. Perhaps you have an email or letter from the person you are angry at or the company that rejected your application. Perhaps you have a ring or picture that symbolizes your relationship with the person with whom you are struggling.

Observe It Safely

- *Put It in a Safe Place:* Begin by holding this object, and let the struggle come to mind. Once you hold it in your mind, I want you to bring it into an imaginary closed room, close the door, and then lock it.
- *Observe It:* Walk around the outside of the locked room and look through the window. Imagine you are spying on the problem. Simply observe it. First, notice what the problem actually is: is it hearing "no," not getting what you want, losing something precious? If defensive, hopeless, or angry thoughts come to mind, just notice them and let them fade away like clouds. Spend some time curiously watching, studying, and getting to know the problem.
- *Garden Walk:* If you feel safe enough and ready, I want you to go to the door and pick up the object. Walk with it to the garden outside. Find a couple of benches nearby and put it on one while you sit on the other. Do not say anything; just sit with the problem for a moment. As you become more comfortable sitting in the presence of the problem, I want you to say to yourself, "I am sitting with what is for the moment. This simply is what is for the moment." Notice how it feels to be with what is.

- *Observe What Arises:* If emotions come up, just let them pass through—knowing each is a guest in your life that will not stay forever. Just be with each new feeling or thought that arises, and then let it go. You may find it helpful to return your focus to your breath if you feel overwhelmed. Do this until the waves of emotion subside.
- *Say Goodbye:* When you are done sitting with the problem, say goodbye as each of you walk down your chosen paths.

Note: If this becomes overwhelming, simply stop. You may need some more time with the issue before you are able to fully experience it. You may also want to try using less emotionally charged problems for this exercise until it becomes easier.

• 5 •

One Bite Is All It Takes

Mindfully Waking Up to Your Life

If you took the opportunity to practice Chocolate Meditation No. 1 or No. 2, you likely noticed that slowing down when you eat chocolate results in a different experience of an otherwise unremarkable everyday activity—and often drastically so. This shift has less to do with slowness per se and more to do with *how* you focus your attention. In these meditations, you are asked to shift your mind from its default setting of judgment and evaluation, which evolved to help early humans to survive. Instead, these meditations encouraged you to simply notice your experience with curiosity. This quality of one's attention is called *mindfulness*, and it is a particularly useful skill for creating extraordinary happiness.

MINDFULNESS

Mindfulness has received significant attention in recent years here in the West. Although we imported the idea more than sixty years ago from Asian Buddhists, it is only in the last few years that it has really caught on with the general public. Why has it become so popular? The answer is simple: Scientific research indicates that mindfulness helps with most common maladies of the twenty-first century—from physical conditions such as diabetes and cancer, to stress, depression, anxiety, and relationship distress. Professionals are now jumping on board with those tie-dyed hippies of the 1960s: There is something to meditation after all.

So, what is mindfulness exactly? Mindfulness (Sanskrit, *smirti*) is a form of attention used in traditional Buddhist meditations and can be found in some form in virtually every human culture. Mindfulness has three essential elements:[1]

1. Self-regulated awareness (focusing the mind intentionally) of a physical or mental experience occurring in the present moment
2. Nonjudgmental observation
3. Accepting "what is" with compassion

Many liken it to experiencing life through the proverbial eyes of a child: fresh, curious, alive, and pure. Often, it involves reexperiencing the familiar as if it were the first time: with curiosity rather than evaluation and judgment. The chocolate meditations have allowed you to mindfully reexperience chocolate: experiencing the colors, sounds, scents, and multifaceted taste. By slowing down and focusing your attention on the fullness of the experience, you were able to have a new experience with a familiar favorite: chocolate.

Mindfulness can be practiced on any object of the mind's attention. Rather than chocolate, traditional Buddhists focus on something that is lower in calories and always with you: the breath. This form of meditation involves watching and noticing the breath as it moves in and out of the body while quieting the mind of inner chatter. Although the instructions seem simple and straightforward, the actual practice is not. If you have ever tried to focus on observing your breath while quieting your thoughts, you will soon discover that within seconds your mind is off and wandering—putting together the grocery list, wondering if you are doing this meditation right, remembering the person you forgot to call today, feeling the ache in your neck, hearing the hum of the air conditioner, or remembering a random argument you had years ago. Typically, the mind jumps from one thought to the next in a wild and inexplicable manner, often referred to as "monkey mind."

After beginning by focusing on your present moment experience (the first element of mindfulness), at some point—seconds or sometimes minutes later—you realize that you are no longer focusing on your breath. At this moment, the other two elements of mindfulness come into play: nonjudgment and compassion. First, refrain from berating yourself and telling yourself what a lousy meditator you are, that there is no hope for you as a meditator, or that this was all a stupid idea. Instead, the task is to be compassionate with yourself and accept that this is what the mind does, and it is OK. For most, this is the hardest part: to be gentle with oneself when the mind wanders off. The fact is that this is how our minds work—until we train our minds to work differently. Once you stop yourself from judgment and instead accept your experience with compassion, you simply return your focus to your breath for the next few seconds before it races off again. Thus, the practice of mindfulness, especially in the beginning, is a back and forth from focusing to losing focus, refocusing and then losing focus again.[2] Meditation is more like a dance that looks this:

WHAT ACTUALLY HAPPENS DURING MINDFULNESS MEDITATION

- Focus—lose focus—gently refocus without judgment.
- Focus—lose focus—gently refocus without judgment.
- Focus—lose focus—gently refocus without judgment.
- Focus—lose focus—gently refocus without judgment.
- Focus—lose focus—gently refocus without judgment.

On the outside people may see a serene picture of a person quietly meditating; on the inside, your mind is bouncing all over the place, much like a ball that has been carefully balanced atop an orange cone but keeps falling off its perch. Each time, you run after it and bring it back to gently place it back on the cone. However, the goal of this game is not what you might assume. The goal is *not* to get the ball to stay on top of the cone forever. Instead, the purpose is to benefit from the exercise you get from running back and forth repeatedly. If you did this in the physical world, you would be getting great aerobic exercise. When you do this in the mental world, your brain gets a workout—that literally changes its physiology the same way aerobic exercise changes the body.

WHAT MINDFULNESS ISN'T

When learning about mindfulness, it is worth noting what mindfulness isn't:

- **Simply a Relaxation Technique:** Although it may lead to reducing stress, mindfulness itself is *not* strictly speaking a technique for relaxation, such as biofeedback. Instead, it is a practice that slowly shifts how you relate to your mind over time. Sometimes when you meditate, you will feel relaxed afterward; other times, you will still feel stressed—and not judging or being frustrated with such meditations is an important part of the practice. Just as you would not expect yourself to suddenly be "in shape" after a single trip to the gym, the effects of mindfulness are cumulative, not a quick fix.

- **Stopping Thoughts:** When most of us in the West learn that the instructions to mindfulness include "quieting inner dialogue and thoughts," we take these instructions quite literally because we have been trained to do so since kindergarten. However, mindfulness is *not* about trying to stop all your thoughts. I have worked with thousands of people who assumed they were "bad" at meditating because they could not stop their thoughts for twenty minutes and therefore stopped practicing. Let's be clear: when all your thoughts stop, you are either dead or in a coma—definitely not the desired result of mindfulness practice. Instead, the goal is to change your relationships to your thoughts, which happens through your efforts to quiet and redirect them, not stop them.

- **Going into a Trance:** Some fear and others hope that mindfulness meditation is a type of trance state that allows you to escape reality for a while or develop special powers, like levitating or telekinesis. For better or worse, mindfulness does none of these things. Instead, if practiced correctly, mindfulness will actually enable you to stay present with realities you would prefer to avoid. However, once you allow yourself to experience painful or frightening realities you prefer to avoid, you will find that your experience of them shifts in ways that open new possibilities for change.

- **Flow State:** I once had a student who claimed that he experienced "mindfulness" when he ran. Although sometimes there is overlap, mindfulness is quite different from a *flow state* such as a "runner's high." A Hungarian-born psychologist, Mihaly Csikszentmihalyi, has spent his career studying flow states, which are moments of optimal experience and highly correlated with happiness.[3] People enter a state of flow when they become joyfully absorbed in a challenging activity in which there is a merging of action and awareness and typically a lack of self-awareness. People often report flow when there is an optimal balance between their skill and the current challenge in activities such as sports, music, art, writing, crafting, gardening, woodworking, cooking, and so forth. Each person experiences flow with different activities. Professional athletes and musicians commonly report flow during games and performances. Scientists and nerdy professors like myself actually experience flow writing reviews of professional literature and doing research, the very activities students complain about. Others use knitting or crafting activities to achieve flow, which doesn't work for me. However, as wonderful as flow is, it is not mindfulness. Some of the distinctions include:

- *Intention:* A person practices mindfulness on purpose and intentionally; the flow state is a by-product of another activity that a person cannot willfully enter.
- *Emotional Outcome:* Flow is defined by a state of joy and happiness; mindfulness may or may not result in any particular state of mind. Not expecting a particular emotional outcome is part of the process.
- *Quality of Awareness:* Flow involves an effortless and almost magical merging of awareness with action, allowing the awareness of self to fade away. Mindfulness demands significant and consistent discipline to quiet the inner chatter, and deliberate effort is always involved. If flow is sounding more inviting than mindfulness about now, don't worry, we will get back to it in chapter 8 when we discuss the gratifications. Both mindfulness and flow play key roles in your future happiness.

IS RELIGION INVOLVED?

Mindfulness as traditionally practiced by Buddhists is not actually a "religious" activity. Buddhists are *atheists*: they do not view Buddha as a god but rather a man who achieved a perfected wisdom into the nature of suffering. Thus, Buddhist mindfulness practices are used as the "entry level" vehicle to psychological knowledge about the nature of suffering and its causes. Rather than a faith-based religion, their approach is most like that of scientists: "Don't believe me. Try it for yourself and see if there is any truth to it." As traditionally practiced, mindfulness is about studying the mind and how it works, particularly as it relates to suffering. So you don't have to know anything about the Buddha to practice meditating; you just have to be willing to get to know your own mind—the good, the bad, and the ugly. All that said, virtually every culture has some version of mindful breath meditation. Judeo-Christian forms of meditation aim to quiet the mind so that the practitioner can directly experience God, another option you may or may not find appealing. In sum, mindfulness is a universal practice that can be purely psychological or that can have a spiritual or religious element.

DOING NOTHING IN A DO-MORE SOCIETY

Paradoxically, although mindfulness is everywhere—the cover of *Time*, schools, hospitals, women's magazines, sports magazines, and so on—it is extremely countercultural. Contemporary society is constantly on the move, valuing stimulation, productivity, goal achievement, excitement, and progress. Sitting in an empty room by yourself watching yourself breathe while quieting your thoughts with no external stimulation does not have the gravitational pull of your friend's latest Instagram post, the next episode of your favorite show, randomly surfing the Internet, or even a full email inbox. Our culture has moved from seeking immediate gratification a decade ago to demanding instant gratification of virtually all whims and needs (notice what happens to your friends, family, and coworkers the next time the Wi-Fi® goes down).

Additionally, although scientists can attest to its negative health effects, in most work contexts, if you don't multitask, you won't make it. Worst of all, mindfulness produces nothing concrete and cannot measurably move you toward your goals. The most difficult part of practicing mindfulness is not quieting your mind, but rather convincing yourself to let go for a few minutes each day of the intense and multifaceted cultural values and beliefs that devalue a practice that looks like "you are doing nothing."

WHY BOTHER MEDITATING?

At this point you may be asking, why bother sitting and watching yourself breathe? That is a good question. Buddhists have done it for more than twenty-five hundred years, and variations of this type of breath meditation can be found in most world religions. For example, Christians practice contemplative prayer, a practice that is gaining increasing popularity in the West in the form of its modern incarnation of centering prayer as described by Father Thomas Keating. Similarly, many synagogues are hosting Kabbalistic meditation for those of Jewish faith. For thousands of years, people around the world have been meditating to get closer to God or to further their spiritual development. I realize that communing with God or achieving enlightenment may not be at the top of your to-do list for today, but these are not the only reasons a person might want to consider starting this new habit. In recent years, Western scientists have discovered that this type of mindfulness meditation has a profound effect on physical and mental health.

Jon Kabat-Zinn has been a leader in bringing the practice of mindfulness to the field of behavioral medicine. He developed his mindfulness-based stress reduction program at the University of Massachusetts's medical center to supplement conventional medical treatment, particularly with patients who were not responding well to such treatments. He began focusing on treating chronic pain, and over the years his program, along with others based on his model, have been used to reduce symptoms in the treatment of a wide range of physical and mental health issues,[4] including:

Physical Disorders that Improve with Mindfulness

- Chronic pain
- Cancer: psychological, biological, and sleep outcomes
- Cardiovascular disorders
- Epilepsy
- HIV/AIDS
- Psoriasis
- Rheumatoid arthritis
- Fibromyalgia
- Organ transplant
- Type II diabetes
- Multiple sclerosis
- Sleep disturbance
- Mixed medical diagnosis

Mental Health Disorders that Improve with Mindfulness

- Depression and depression relapse
- Bipolar disorder
- Anxiety and panic disorders

- Substance use disorders
- Eating disorders
- Borderline personality
- ADD or ADHD (attention deficit/hyperactivity disorder)
- Oppositional and conduct issues
- Trauma and PTSD (post-traumatic stress disorder)
- Sexual abuse
- Psychosis

And if you are one of the lucky few who has never experienced anything on these lists, researchers report that regular mindfulness is helpful for general psychological and relational wellness.

Psychological Benefits of Mindfulness

- Increased positive emotion and well-being
- Reduced stress
- Increased emotional regulation
- Increased metacognitive awareness
- Decreased rumination
- Improved attention
- Increased acceptance and decreased avoidance
- Clarification of values
- Increased self-compassion

Relational Benefits of Mindfulness

- Increased marital satisfaction
- Increased empathy and compassion
- Increased acceptance of self and partner
- Increased awareness of interactional patterns
- Increased ability to respond with awareness
- Greater sense of freedom and safety in relationships
- Greater sense of unity and separation

Thus, much of the fervor around mindfulness has been generated by the impressive research findings on the many measurable benefits of mindfulness. But how does mindfulness work? Prior to mindfulness, there was no existing medical or psychological intervention that could possibly treat so many different disorders. So, what is going on here? Summed up in three words: the stress response.

THE STRESS RESPONSE: MEET YOUR INNER LIZARD

Mindfulness appears to be the cure-all snake oil of the twenty-first century, until you factor in the level of stress that characterizes life today. Virtually all physical and mental issues that commonly plague us today are either caused or exacerbated by stress. A rapidly growing body of research documents that mindfulness is one of the most efficient and effective means of reducing a person's daily level of stress.

The stress response—or fight-flight-freeze response—is one of the most important and impressive features of our human anatomy.[5] Dan Siegel's "handy model" of the brain is my favorite method of explaining the stress response, even if it does not fully capture the astounding complexity of the human brain that researchers discover more about each day.[6] Please pick a hand and follow along (you may also visit www .mindfulnessforchocolatelovers.com for a video demonstration):

- **Built-In Model:** Make a fist with your thumb hidden under your fingers (note: this is not the same fist used in self-defense, as you'd likely break your thumb). This is your built-in model of your brain.
- **Brain Stem at Your Wrist:** Your wrist represents the brain stem, the oldest part of the brain that keeps your heart beating and lungs working without you having to think about it. We don't have conscious control of this part of our brain. Traditional models of the brain referred to this as the reptilian part of the brain, but contemporary researchers have demonstrated that reptile brains are slightly more complex.
- **Limbic System in Your Thumb:** Your thumb, which should be tightly wrapped under your fingers in this model, represents the limbic system, which is the center of the stress response. This part of the brain is designed for physical survival: fighting a bear (or another predator), outrunning a bear, or hiding from a bear by freezing like a statue. If we want to get technical, there is also the "faint" response, where you play dead. This is the part of

the brain that takes over when we believe we are under threat, which is essential for surviving physical life threats. Although not technically the reptilian part of the brain, its function is beautifully exemplified by a lizard in your yard: Even when it seems to be peacefully sunning itself, it is nonetheless on constant high alert and bolts with the smallest threat, including a leaf falling gently nearby. Your inner lizard's ceaseless motto: safety first.

- **Prefrontal Knuckles:** The knuckles that are wrapped over your thumb represent your prefrontal cortex, the part of the brain that houses all that we think of as what makes us "human" as well as "uniquely ourselves." This part of the brain is responsible for language, logic, creativity, and good decision making. When I teach mindfulness to children, we call this the "smart part" of the brain, needed to focus in class, do math, read, and make good decisions.

The prefrontal cortex is also the only part of the brain that can quiet the lower limbic and reptile-like parts of the brain. For example, before the prefrontal cortex has time to process whether the wiggly thing in our path is a deadly snake or a rope, a five-bell alarm has been set by our limbic system, priming the body to fight, run, or freeze to ensure survival. Humans with lightning-fast limbic systems survive better; thus, our limbic systems are much faster than our prefrontal cortexes. But once the prefrontal cortex evaluates the situation using logic and reasoning to determine that the wiggly thing is actually a rope, it turns on the relaxation response, which is a true physiological response that is the opposite of the stress response. Please note that a margarita on the beach is *not* the same thing as the relaxation response, which is a natural physiological process with its own set of hormones and biomarkers that counterbalances the stress response and brings the prefrontal cortex back online. In contrast, alcohol shuts down parts of the prefrontal cortex, which is why driving and decision making are impaired. In fact, for some, alcohol seems to let the inner lizard out to run wild.

STRESS: FLIPPING YOUR LID

If you go back to the handy model of the brain and lift your four fingers to reveal your thumb underneath, this is what Dan Siegel refers to as "flipping your lid." When you flip your lid—bing!—your inner lizard takes over and your prefrontal cortex goes offline to one degree or another. The more stressed you are, the more your higher brain functions are temporarily shut down. A good example of a small flip is being annoyed with your partner and making an edgy comment, whereas a major flipping of the lid may include yelling, slamming doors, name calling, saying things you don't mean, and wanting to break up. The prefrontal cortex can consciously shut down the stress response once it realizes the danger is over, such as confirming that you just saw a rope, not a snake. *Regular mindfulness practice enables a person to consciously choose to shut down the stress response.*

TRAUMA AND MINDFULNESS

Mindfulness has also been used to help address negative brain patterns associated with trauma. A healthy brain frequently spends time in a state of *neural integration*, which is associated with bodily and emotional regulation, empathy and attuned communication, and the regulation of stress.[7] Think of it as firing on all cylinders: All parts of your brain are working together harmoniously.

However, trauma interferes with neural integration. During a traumatic experience, people flip their lids so that they can fight, run, or freeze to survive. Once in the stress state for survival, the body can hear and see better. In addition, all the blood is moved from non-survival needs—such as digestion, immunity, and reproduction—to the muscles so a person can fight or run. After all, you don't need to worry about absorbing nutrients in your lunch, fighting a virus, or planning a baby room when a saber-toothed tiger is about to eat you for supper. But this does explain why stomach, immunity, muscular, and fertility issues are common with people whose stress response is turned on more than twenty minutes per month—about the same amount of time that leading evolutionary biologists believe early humans were engaged in fights for survival.

Once the stress response is triggered during a traumatic crisis, the hippocampus goes offline with the prefrontal cortex. The hippocampus works somewhat like a video recorder that integrates memories of your senses—sight, smell, taste, feel, and sound—into a coherent narrative or story, which becomes the memory of the event. Thus, the hippocampus does not make a video of the traumatic memory, and the various bits of experience get stored in implicit memory rather than the normal memory narrative. Implicit memory does not make distinctions such as time and place, and when these memories are triggered, it feels like memory is happening in the here and now. That is what we call a flashback: an old memory gets replayed and feels as if it is happening in the present. In neurological terms, the treatment of trauma involves reintegrating the implicit memories of the events in order to create a coherent narrative of the event. Once the trauma event is fully re-storied, the person can recall the trauma without flipping his or her lid.

RELAXATION RESPONSE AND BREATH

The physiological opposite of the stress response is the relaxation response, which not only turns off the stress response but also puts the body in a neutral state again. One of the most direct ways to trigger the relaxation response is to focus on your breath. Why? Because your breath is predictable: it goes in, it goes out, it goes in and then out again. When the external world is highly predictable, the brain sends a message that you are safe and shuts down the stress alarm. Thus, when you focus on your breath, your brain quickly sends the message that you are safe and triggers relaxation.

REFOCUSING TO REWIRE YOUR BRAIN

When most people learn mindfulness, they logically assume that longer periods without thoughts are better than losing focus and then refocusing. If you are meditating for spiritual enlightenment or communion with God, longer periods without thoughts are better. However, *if you want psychological benefits such as reducing stress or ADHD symptoms, losing focus and then refocusing is where the action—rewiring your brain—happens.*

The "therapy" that results from practicing mindfulness comes from interrupting the wandering mind and bringing it back to focus.

Each time we do this, we appear to be strengthening the ability of the higher centers of the brain to override the reactivity of lower centers, specifically the limbic system, which regulates the stress response or fight-flight-freeze mechanism.

Recent brain research by Richard Davidson at the University of Wisconsin indicates that after as little as eight weeks, people who begin meditating start to see this type of change in brain functioning.[8] Regular practice—but not necessarily sporadic practice—actually "rewires" your brain, literally changing its physical and chemical structure. These changes seem to be changing a person's entire disposition: general mood, attitude, and sense of well-being. That is powerful stuff. What is even more exciting is that research indicates that what mindfulness does to your brain is quite different from what medications like antidepressants do to your brain. Antidepressants calm the reactive, emotional parts of the middle brain. Mindfulness, on the other hand, actually "strengthens" (increases activity in) the parts of the brain that are related to compassion and positive mood—resulting in, you guessed it—greater happiness—and not just happier moods, but a happier disposition or personality.

Mindfulness Effects on the Brain

- Increased gray matter density in the prefrontal cortex, the part of the brain associated with language, executive function (ability to manage self and achieve goals), mood regulation, and so on.[9]
- Improved attentional processing.[10]
- Increased gray matter of the hippocampus, the part of the brain associated with memory.[11]
- Decreased gray matter density of the amygdala, the part of the brain related to the stress response.[12] Since you are not using your stressed-out brain, you lose it! A good thing in this case.
- Increased gray matter in the brain stem, which is related to the relaxation response.[13]

I am hoping that you are getting excited about the possibility of training your brain to be a happy brain—with or without chocolate!

THE MINDFUL MIND

What is the difference between a mind on mindfulness compared to everyday thinking? When practicing mindfulness, the mind is:

- **Focused:** Often people think that meditation is "relaxing," not requiring much effort or work, but in fact, it requires substantial concentrated effort. It is an exercise in focusing the mind. You may feel more relaxed afterward, and sometimes during, but it is not to be confused with relaxing at the beach or in front of your favorite screen.
- **Receptive:** During mindfulness meditation, the mind is receptive, open to what is. There is not an attempt to change anything—including your breath—visualize anything, or do anything. The idea is to sit with what is, even if it is unpleasant.
- **Fully Present:** Mindfulness meditation is perhaps one of the purest forms of being fully present in the moment. You are not thinking about the past or future, just this one moment—nothing more and nothing less.
- **Nonjudgmental:** We all like to think that we are "nonjudgmental," but in fact our brains are hard-wired to make judgments. For better or worse, the only way for the brain to take in any information is to notice differences: in temperature, color, form, movement, and so forth. If there is no difference, no information comes in. All differences are evaluated against "known dangers" in the limbic part of the brain, which responds before we are even conscious of what we are seeing. So the brain is constantly noting differences and making judgments about danger. Our job in meditation is to observe this process and refrain from allowing our higher minds and personalities to add any judgment to the basic process of noticing differences.
- **Gentle and Kind:** Perhaps the most important part of mindfulness is to be kind and gentle with yourself. Mindfulness often brings up some of our less-than-enlightened qualities: difficulty focusing, embarrassing emotions, and unwanted thoughts. In these moments, your most important task is to be kind to yourself—rather than judgmental, punitive, or frustrated. This is often harder than focusing—and therefore all the more important.

FLAVORS OF MINDFULNESS

Like chocolate, mindfulness comes in many flavors, shapes, and forms—
so surely you will find one that suits your tastes.

- **Samatha:** The most basic Buddhist mindfulness meditation is referred to as *samatha*. Samatha involves a single focus, such as watching your breath, saying a mantra, or eating chocolate—OK, the latter is not traditional, but it still counts. This is usually the first type of mindfulness meditation a person learns. You can find a guided version of samatha at www.mindfulnessforchoco latelovers.com.
- **Vipassana:** *Vipassana* is the other common form of Buddhist mindfulness meditation. In vipassana, the focus is simply watching the mind's moment-to-moment experiencing. The field of awareness is wide open: observing all stimuli—sounds, thoughts, sensations, emotions—move through your consciousness like clouds across the sky. This form of meditation is usually taught after samatha.
- **Christian Variations:** Though less well known, Christians have a meditation tradition, which has several parallels with the Buddhist tradition. Christian contemplative prayer makes a distinction similar to samatha versus vipassana in the Buddhist tradition. In the Christian meditative tradition, one can concentrate on either a single focus, such as breath, or a word, such as God, Christ, or Holy Spirit; this is the same as samatha. Alternatively, one can simply quiet the mind so that God, the divine presence, can be experienced directly without language or imagery, remarkably similar to vipassana.
- **Mindfulness Walking Meditation:** Walking meditation involves mindfully walking. Similar to eating, you greatly slow down the typical pace: each step can take over a minute, so you do not need a lot of space. You bring attention to the sensation of your heel then toes as they slowly meet the earth, noticing how your foot feels, how your weight and balance shift, and how all parts of your body move. Typically, the "walk" consists of tracing your steps back and forth over the same five- to ten-foot stretch of the living room, office floor, or garden path.

Just remember to keep your eyes open for this meditation so you do not fall.

- **Mindful Body Scan:** Unlike traditional behavioral psychology body scans that require you to relax parts of your body, a mindful body scan *does not require you to relax any part of your body.* Instead, you mindfully, nonjudgmentally, and compassionately notice sensations in your body. You can begin with your head or your feet, and slowly move your attention to each major body part, noticing any and all sensations, such as the temperature of the room, texture of clothing, physical pain, discomfort, tension, relaxation, lack of any sensation, etc. As you notice these sensations, try to quiet the mind when it tries to judge them as good or bad, desired or undesired. If there is a particularly difficult sensation such as pain, try to become curious about it, noticing its qualities, movement, and subtle shifts. The task is to simply notice with curiosity and compassion. You can find a guided version of the body scan at www.mindfulnessforchocolatelovers.net.

- **Focusing on Bodily Sensations:** When you are struggling with pain, an itch, or other strong bodily sensations, you may want to switch your focus from your breath to the bodily sensation, bringing curiosity and mindful awareness to the experience. This is particularly poignant for those with chronic pain. For years, I had terrible neck pain; each time it hit, I would think, "there it is again," and immediately my mind would race off with woeful thoughts, which only made things worse. When I began greeting the pain with mindful awareness, I began to realize it was multifaceted: the location would shift ever so slightly; the intensity would wax and wane; there were tight spots that had a different quality of pain. Suddenly, the pain in my neck had as many phases as the moon, and I could appreciate the less intense moments even within a "bad episode." The more I made peace with my pain, the less it seemed to hurt. I should mention that this is different from the "relaxation" meditations where the practitioner tries to relax the tense muscle. Instead, mindfulness is just about curiously observing "what is" rather than trying to relax or intervene on the pain. By just observing, you shift your relationship to it, resulting in the proverbial "attitude adjustment."

- **Focusing on Emotions and Thoughts:** When you have particular thoughts or emotions that are troublesome or constantly interrupt your meditation, you can choose to mindfully engage them, similar to how you worked with bodily sensations. Again, the idea is not to change, but rather to observe the emotion or thought. Where do you feel it in your body? What are its qualities: hot, tight, piercing, dull, lifeless? Does it have color? Do images come attached to it? Do other thoughts and feelings come along? Sit back and watch how the drama unfolds in your body and mind. I promise you, it is quite a show. The next time you feel stressed out, angry, or hopeless, take a seat and watch. I often find that my mind in these states is like a pinball machine: thoughts and emotions bouncing from point to point, setting off lights, bells, and whistles, and moving faster than I can keep up with. If you stay focused on observing your mind do its crazy dance rather than join in, it will eventually stop. And, wow, will it feel good. Often, days of stewing can be resolved in minutes of quietly observing all that the mind wants to think and feel. You will be back for more—I promise.
- **Spiritual Development:** If you choose to use mindfulness meditation as a vehicle for your spiritual development rather than the physical and emotional benefits researchers have documented, then the length of time you can maintain your focus is more crucial. When the mind is still, the divine makes itself known and you fall in rhythm with the cosmos. This has been the primary goal of most meditators in the past, but this does not have to be yours—or perhaps you will find over time that you want to approach meditation with this in mind.

ENEMY NO. 1: PERFECTION

If you are still looking for an enemy from the last chapter, you are sure to find one in meditation: perfectionism. When most of us sit down to do mindfulness with a breath focus for the first time, we tend to make it a violent act. We listen to the seemingly simple instructions to focus on our breath and assume that it is pretty easy. We quietly tell ourselves, "Others may have a problem, but this sounds easy enough. I am sure I can do this." But we soon discover that after five seconds our mind is wandering. When we eventually notice that in the space of five seconds we have had two internal arguments—one with our spouse, the other our coworker, planned the meals for the week, and found the answer to world peace rather than focus on our breath, we then start to berate ourselves: "What's wrong with me? Why can't I focus for five seconds? I must not be doing this right. No one else seems to be having this problem. It must be me." Sound familiar? So it is critical that kindness be a part of the process. Each time we catch our mind wandering, we need to return to our focus gently, kindly, and lovingly.

For some, being kind to yourself will be more of a challenge than keeping your focus. If you tend to be hard on yourself, this may be the case for you. Keep this in mind with your first attempt. So, enough theory. Let's try this.

MINDFULNESS BREATH MEDITATION

You can use the guided meditation at www.mindfulnessforchocolatelovers.com or use this meditation guide.

Take a Seat

Take a comfortable seat. If you can, sit toward the end of a firm chair so that your back is comfortably erect yet relaxed in posture, without leaning on the chair back. If that isn't comfortable, sit back and relax.

Set a Timer

Use a timer or meditation app, and set it for two to five minutes. This reduces the anxiety of knowing when to stop; the timer will tell you.

Watch Yourself Breathe

Try to quiet your thoughts and focus on your breath. You may choose to focus on how your abdomen rises and falls or where the cool air goes in and out of your nostrils. Just watch and observe your natural breath—however it moves today. Do not try to change its rhythms, depth, or pacing. Just simply watch it.

Lose Focus and Refocus

When you notice your mind wandering, gently bring your attention back to your breath. Remember to do so with compassion. You may say, "Ah, yes, this too," and label the thoughts as "worry," "planning," "emotion," and so on. Then just let the thoughts go like a child releasing a balloon in the air. Continue this ebb and flow of focus-distraction-focus-distraction until the bell rings, knowing that each time you refocus, you rewire your brain.

MINDFULNESS IN EVERYDAY LIFE

Mindfulness can also be practiced with everyday activities. These are some of my favorites.

Mindful Waiting

So how does mindfulness make a difference in our experience of happiness? I live in the greater Los Angeles area. Traffic is common around here. It is a source of much unhappiness for many of us because it seems to impinge upon our time schedules. However, that is only one way to look at traffic. It also can be an opportunity to simply have some downtime. There is nothing you can do when you are parked on the 405 Freeway, even if you drive a commercial version of a military vehicle. But you can choose how you think about it.

You can get angry and throw a fit, much like I did when I was a child and someone stole my chocolate, or you can choose to be with what is: which in this moment is sitting in your car, which is moving down the freeway very, very, very slowly. When I choose to mindfully notice what is going on, I take note that I am sitting comfortably, protected from the elements. My favorite music is readily available, and I am free to sing along. I usually have a mug full of tea to sip if my throat gets hoarse from singing. I like to take in the sunshine and feel the breeze blowing by. And, yes, there may be people waiting for me somewhere in the world, but they are also generally in a safe place and know my circumstances.

One of my more humbling lessons in recent years has come from using my car's navigation system, which tracks the estimated time of arrival with and without traffic. I was surprised to discover how little time I actually lost stuck in traffic. In fact, in many cases I still arrived at the original estimated arrival time, forcing me to realize how pointless my typical stewing and fretting over traffic actually was.

Dishwashing Meditation

I am one of those people who loves to cook but hates to do the dishes. Like most forms of cleaning, dishwashing does not leave me with a great sense of satisfaction or productivity: I just got things back to the same old, same old—whereas when cooking I actually create something new. That is why I really got into dishwashing meditation, which Thich Nhat Hanh describes in his book *Peace Is Every Step*.[14]

As you may be able to guess at this point, dishwashing meditation is a mindfulness exercise where you learn to pay attention to what you are doing, experiencing, and seeing while doing dishes. You mindfully notice the sensations of warm water, soap bubbles, and water on your hands. You notice the curve of each item, the nicks and dings that are its history, its weight and texture. It becomes a meditation of sorts.

Thich Nhat Hanh's idea has radically transformed my relationship to dishwashing. It is now a somewhat indulgent opportunity for me to slow down and reconnect with life. It is a tool for promoting extraordinary happiness. For better or worse, I get several chances every day to practice it! Some days I do more dishwashing meditation than any other form of meditation.

Interestingly, the practice has spread to other areas. Now, any time I feel water run over my hands, I am reminded to be mindful in that moment. Each time I wash my hands at work, at a restaurant, or at home, I am reminded to be mindful and get a mini-break from the day's hassles and concerns. I am often asked how as a psychotherapist I manage to listen to people's problems hour after hour. Would you believe washing my hands helps?

Yoga and the Breathing Pretzel

If you have ever been in a yoga class, you know. The teacher calls out something like, "I now want you try to move your right leg as close to your left ear as possible while you then move your left arm behind your back and grab your right foot." Your arms are flailing, you fall over, and wonder what is going on. Who is crazier—the teacher or you for taking the class? But that is missing the point.

The point of yoga is not to get good at imitating pretzels. The point is to breathe: to breathe in those very moments when your body and mind want to tense up, give up, or give out. When you push your body to its edge—the point where it can stretch no further and the mind says you have gone too far—that is when you need to breathe and mindfully experience the tension—to feel the tightness in your body, to feel the muscles working, to feel your heart beating, to notice your mind's inner chitter-chatter that says you cannot do this, to feel the emotions of frustration, anger, and fear—watching it all move across your mind and body like clouds across the sky—and to keep breathing. It is mindfulness in full motion. And you do it not to get your foot behind your ear but so that when you are off your yoga mat and life throws itself into pretzel-like knots—your child throws a fit at a fancy restaurant, your colleague fails to follow through on his half of the project, your spouse is in a foul mood—you can keep breathing.

Water Meditation

Both the landline and mobile phones are ringing at the same time; I hear the computer's bell chiming, letting me know more email has arrived; I have one graduate student in my office with a pickle of a problem; I have a line of students forming outside my door with questions and concerns; and then my colleague pops his head into my office to let me know he is on his way to our faculty meeting and that he will see me there—I might be a couple of minutes late. This is not life in a Zen monastery but the ivory tower and similar places where most of us work and live. And, quite honestly, I think mindfulness should be a requisite in the latter more than the former.

I take a deep breath, and it helps. I make arrangements with the students to continue the conversation. I let the phones go to voicemail and refrain from checking the latest email. And then I take thirty seconds to myself before I run off to my meeting. The ultimate mini-mindfulness break: a sip of water. I close my eyes and focus on fully experiencing the taste and feel of water. It is cool on my tongue. But the taste—I am at a loss for words. How do you describe the taste of water? I laugh to myself. This ironically makes the mindful experience all the more pure and simple. One more sip, and this time it is easier to do so with a quiet mind. The email bell rings again, my reminder that the meditation is over. I am off to my meeting—with a clear enough head for the next adventure of the day.

This is my favorite busy day meditation. I use it during my most challenging professional meetings as well as when I have more errands than time. More than any other technique I have ever tried, water medi-tation quiets my mind the fastest. The practice simply involves mindfully drinking water, the same way you have learned to mindfully eat choco-late. If you happen to have a glass of life's essential elixir nearby, simply take a sip and notice the quality of its taste. For me, and many others, no words come. My mind becomes suddenly quiet and peaceful—the closest thing to Zen "sudden enlightenment" that I have ever experienced. Even though water has been considered "tasteless" for centuries, scientists at the California Institute of Technology have recently determined that humans have some sort of specific taste sensor for water that is distinct from other taste buds.[15] Perhaps you can practice discovering it yourself.

Any-Sense-Will-Do Meditation

The reason you meditate or do yoga or pray is not so much that it feels great in the moment. The real reason is that you need the practice to be able to handle life's difficult moments. Practice creates habits. When you are under stress, you revert to your habits—so make sure that you cultivate some good ones. The practice of mindfulness allows you to take anything in your external or internal environment and use it to calm and focus the mind. When life starts to spiral out of control, you can choose to focus on any one of your senses, and mindfully taste, feel, hear, see, or smell what is in the moment. Close your eyes and feel the breeze on your face (one of my absolute favorites); listen to the sounds surrounding you; feel the ground under your feet or the chair you are sitting on; notice just the colors and shapes in front of you; drink in the subtle scents that surround you—the ones you never notice ordinarily. Your mind will be different. Your day will be different. You will become skilled at finding happiness in any moment. You are learning the secrets of extraordinary happiness.

"I'D LOVE TO BUT. . . .": FAVORITE EXCUSES FOR AVOIDING REGULAR MEDITATION

"I've Got No Time"

Lots of people think meditating sounds like a good idea—in theory. But most everyone says, "I do not have time for one more thing in my schedule." You may not have time for the commonly recommended twenty to forty minutes per day—especially at first. But *everyone* can carve out one to five minutes a day. That is all you need to start. The trick is to make it a *habit*. The best way to do that is to attach it to another habit that you do every day: showering, brushing your teeth, eating a meal, working out, waking up, going to bed, drinking a cup of coffee, or commuting.

Then dedicate one to five minutes before or after one of these activities to meditate every day. After two to three weeks it will feel strange to not meditate. It is quite simple and does not take much effort.

In fact, it is best to think of mindfulness like flossing your teeth: you will rarely *feel* like doing it, but you know you have to do it anyway. On most days, it will feel like a boring chore—not some mystical, spiritual, spa-like activity. It's disciplined. It's tedious. It's repetitive. It's dull. It's monotonous. If there is the slightest bit of stress or time pressure, your inner lizard will really fight you on it. But that is when you go into fierce negotiations for one to two minutes with that little guy. You always have sixty seconds. Like flossing, which apparently reduces heart disease and diabetes, the rewards are remarkable. In the case of mindfulness, you literally rewire your brain and open your life to new levels of happiness and joy. But you will have to wrestle with your lizard on a regular basis to reap the benefits.

EXERCISE: FINDING THE TIME TO BREATHE

Download worksheet at www.mindfulnessforchocolate.com.

Identify three daily tasks/times that you think might be good to pair with a one- to five-minute meditation:

1.

2.

3.

Choose which you would like to try first as an activity to "pair" with mindfulness and try it for a week. If you are able to make it work for at least four or five days that week, keep going. If not, try the next activity on the list. Continue until you find a good five minutes of your day to practice mindfulness. Do not be surprised if you decide to go a little longer some days.

Reminder

Once you select an activity/day/time, set a reminder on a digital device that will be with you when you plan to practice.

Keeping Time

It is helpful to find a way to time your one to five minutes, such as an app or the built-in timer on your phone. Apps such as InsightTimer or HeadSpace include guided meditations as well.

"I'm Not Good at It"

Anyone in a conscious state who is breathing can practice mindfulness. Remember, the task is not to keep yourself from thinking. The task is to *return your focus* to your breath when—not if—the mind wanders, which it will over and over and over again. Especially for those new to mindfulness, it is returning to your focus that is the most beneficial part. Some days your mind may wander for the entire five-minute period; thankfully you have the bell to remind you to stop. So, you did it! You were able to return your focus to your breath—even once makes a difference. The next day you may be able to do it two, four, twenty times. Each day is different.

You will notice you will become a good weather forecaster, becoming intimately aware of your inner weather: stormy days, sunny days, cloudy days, snow, hail, thunder, rainbows. A five-minute mindfulness practice at the beginning of each day gives you a good sense of what lies ahead—perhaps giving you warning as to whether you need to bring an umbrella or even stay home. When I find myself unable to focus as I normally do because I am distracted with the day's itinerary, it is a clear sign that I should cancel whatever is not essential to keep from flipping my lid.

"I Am Not the Type"

I've heard it from plenty of people: "I am not the meditating type." Let's think about this. What makes one the meditating type? Research indicates that anyone who has a brain will benefit. I am hoping that includes you. You do not need to join a monastery, sit for hours on end, wear strange robes, burn incense, or chant in a foreign language. You simply need to pay attention to your breath for a few minutes each day. You are free to be your wild, crazy, fun-loving, chocolate-nibbling self the rest of the day. So, this is for everybody—or at least anybody who seeks more happiness in life.

MINDFULNESS RESOURCES

Mindfulness Training Programs and Resources

- Book website: www.mindfulnessforchocolatelovers.com
- Author website: www.dianegehart.com
- Mindfulness-Based Stress Reduction (University of Massachusetts): www.umassmed.edu/cfm.
- Mindfulness Awareness Practices (UCLA): http://marc.ucla.edu/
- Christian Centering Prayer: www.contemplativeprayer.org, www.centeringprayer.org, and www.contemplativeoutreach.org
- Jewish-based meditation: www.awakenedheartproject.org
- Mindfulness in Schools: www.mindfulschool.net

Mindfulness Apps

Here are some of the current popular apps:

- Insight Timer: www.insighttimer.com. Customizable gong timer with thousands of free guided meditations with hundreds of options, such as meditations for sleep, children, and anxiety.
- Headspace: www.headspace.com. A friendly introduction to basic mindfulness practice that many teens and adults enjoy.
- Calm: www.calm.com. Mindfulness with an emphasis on relaxation and sleep.

With or Without Nuts?

Crazy Wisdom and the Back Door to Happiness

A few years back, I was invited to conduct a four-day training for German thera-pists. On the last night, we celebrated with a fabulous dinner at a local restaurant where the tables appeared to be set for Wonderland's Queen of Hearts: the walls were boldly painted red, each chair's shape was reminiscent of card suits, the table was decked with geometric-shaped objects, and mirrors and sheer curtains created optical illusions. The night was filled with good food, great conversation, and much laughter. Wanting to cap the joy-filled evening off with my favorite indulgence—chocolate— I hailed the waiter in my best German. He responded with a negative. I assumed that he had not understood my American accent, so I asked my German colleague to help me translate. The waiter their explained that they had no chocolate desserts: no chocolate torte, no chocolate cakes, no chocolate ice cream, not even a cookie— nichts, nein, keine (so many ways to say "no" in German, and he used them all).

My American brain required a few moments to process this reality: How is it possible that a fine German restaurant has not one morsel of chocolate in the house? My romantic and chocolate-filled vision of Europe came crashing down like a triple scoop of ice cream in the hands of a toddler. As if that were not bad enough, several at the conference offered to run to the local *Tankstelle* (gas station) to get me some chocolate. I refused. To come to the source of the world's finest chocolate and leave with a kid's candy bar was too much to bear.

As we drove home, my hosts and I identified places that would surely have had the divine European chocolate experience I craved—if they were still open. In my mind, I could see the fine torte with more layers than I could count, a thick layer of ganache all around, topped with a chocolate mini-sculpture too beautiful to eat. I obviously had a preconceived notion of what I wanted. But what I got was even better: My romantic stereotype of Europe was shattered, allowing me to fully experience this moment as it was. We laughed wholeheartedly the entire way home about my quest for chocolate—it became a mythic journey by the end of the night. I made friends that night that I have to this day. Although no chocolate passed my lips that night, it was one of the best chocolate experiences of my life.

Much like Alice herself, my trip to wonderland shattered a set of expectations built up over a lifetime while opening my world and my heart to a previously unimagined form of joy, fun, and connection. And, although the challenged beliefs may seem silly and trivial on one level, the experience of being able to gracefully have one's "mind blown" provides practice for navigating more difficult moments in life.

CRAZY WISDOM

At this point, you are probably wondering why the initial text of this chapter is upside down. Hint: It is not an error. Those around you are probably wondering why you are reading your book upside down. My question is: Who is laughing harder? I hope you are. It feels good to be out of the box. Life seems lighter; you laugh more. All problems seem surmountable. This is the joy that comes from crazy wisdom.

If mindfulness is the direct road to reducing the attachments that perpetuate suffering, crazy wisdom is the back door. Crazy wisdom plays with opposites and logic to cut through the assumptions that keep us imprisoned by our attachments and enables us to break loose from our habitual ways of thinking. It shakes up your typical thought patterns, wakes you up, and opens your mind to new possibilities. Nothing is sacred, and everything is sacred all at the same time. The moment you stop taking yourself and life so seriously, you can more authentically and freely embrace life as it is—with all of its paradox, mysteries, darkness, and light. Crazy wisdom allows you to keep laughing through good times and bad, through delays, failure, roadblocks, and your worst fears come true. Crazy wisdom is one of the keys to extraordinary happiness.

SERIOUSLY FUNNY: THE SCIENCE OF HUMOR

For psychologists researching laughter, crazy wisdom is no laughing matter. Although they have taken a measured interest in the effects of humor only in the past couple of decades, evidence is quickly accumulating that the ability to regularly appreciate life's lighter side greatly enhances one's physical and emotional well-being. Researchers at the University of Victoria in Canada found that female executives who used humor to cope with daily hassles had higher self-esteem, less emotional exhaustion, and reduced physical illness.[1] Similarly, in a study at the University of North Carolina, industrial psychologists found that when employees use humor, their performance improves, they experience greater job satisfaction, there is greater team cohesion, they are healthier, and they cope better with stress.[2] When managers are able to laugh often, their subordinates also perform better and evaluate their supervisor's performance higher, and there is greater cohesion. Examining outcomes for trauma survivors, a team of European researchers found that humor was one of the most effective coping strategies for those affected by trauma.[3] When examining long-term marital happiness, communication researchers found that couples who regularly shared laughs while engaging in enjoyable activities were more satisfied with their relationships and more likely to use positive (i.e., nonaggressive) forms of humor with their partners.[4]

NOT ALL HUMOR HELPS

Not all forms of humor are associated with positive outcomes. Psychologists at the University of London have developed a widely used scale, the Humor Style Questionnaire, to study different forms of humor.[5] They identify two positive styles of humor and two negative:

- **Affiliative Humor:** A likely trait of your funniest friends, affiliative humor is used to amuse others and build relationships in a benevolent, kind manner. Individuals who score high in this style of humor tend to tell jokes spontaneously, engage in witty banter, and invoke crazy wisdom to ease social tension. *Examples of items measuring affiliative humor:*
  - I enjoy making people laugh.
  - I don't have to work very hard at making other people laugh—I seem to be a naturally humorous person.

- **Self-Enhancing Humor:** Always able to see the silver lining, persons scoring high in self-enhancing humor use humor to cope with difficulty and stress and have a good-natured attitude toward life and its absurdities. They are masters at crazy wisdom. *Examples of items measuring self-enhancing humor:*

- ○ My humorous outlook on life keeps me from getting overly upset or depressed about things.
- ○ When telling jokes or saying funny things, I am usually not very concerned about how other people are taking it.

- **Aggressive Humor:** Characteristic of some of the least favorite characters in most of our lives, those who use aggressive humor are sarcastic and their "jokes" are intended to manipulate or insult others. Racist and sexist comments often fall into this category. Such individuals are more neurotic and less happy than those using the first two styles. *Examples of items measuring aggressive humor:*

  - ○ If someone makes a mistake, I often tease them about it.
  - ○ Sometimes I think of something that is so funny that I can't stop myself from saying it, even if it is not appropriate for the situation.

- **Self-Defeating Humor:** People who use self-defeating humor put themselves down excessively to ingratiate themselves to others or as a form of defense to hide negative feelings about themselves. Although self-defeating humor can be used to strengthen relationships, it is always at the individual's expense. Persons who score high on this style of humor tend to have higher levels of depression, anxiety, and psychiatric symptoms and lower levels of self-esteem and well-being. *Examples of items measuring self-defeating humor:*

  - ○ Letting others laugh at me is my way of keeping my friends and family in good spirits.
  - ○ I often go overboard in putting myself down when I am making jokes or trying to be funny.

Greater well-being is associated with the first two styles of humor, whereas reduced well-being is associated with the latter two.[6] Furthermore, greater capacity for intimacy is associated with higher affiliative humor and lower self-defeating humor.[7]

You can take the entire test online at http://www.psytoolkit.org/ survey-library/humor-hsq.html.

BUDDHIST CRAZY WISDOM

In the Buddhist world, meditation is the logical, slow-and-steady-wins-the-race approach; crazy wisdom is the wild, off-road shortcut.[8] Crazy wisdom teachings are less commonly imported to the West. This may be because they are so much harder to teach, grasp, and practice. Or perhaps our cultural preference for logical, step-by-step instructions makes the wisdom of the absurd less palatable. However, I believe it is critical to combine the logical, disciplined approach to happiness—meditation—with the backdoor approach of crazy wisdom. Otherwise, you risk making yourself really crazy. As you can see below, a balanced life requires both conventional and crazy wisdom. Trying to live life with only one or the other results in an imbalance. Anyone who makes it a rigid pattern to favor one form of wisdom over another inevitably ends up lost on the search for happiness, likely with health problems, mental health issues, or both.

COMPARING CONVENTIONAL AND CRAZY WISDOM

Conventional Wisdom	Crazy Wisdom
Serious and adult	Playful and childlike
Logical knowing	Intuitive or "heart" knowing
Establishes and reinforces convention	Challenges convention; rebellious
Common sense	Out-of-the-box thinking
Dualistic (either/or) thinking	Non-dualistic (both/and) thinking
Rejects paradox	Trusts paradox
Makes assertions	Questions everything
Takes self and others very seriously	Does not take self or others seriously
Prefers politeness to the truth	Prefers truth to politeness
Great love for a given culture/society	Great love for all of humanity
Fears what is different	Fears nothing
Delights in similarity	Delights in opposites
Planful and calculated	Spontaneous and untamed
Science	Arts
Past and/or future focus	Present focus

CRAZY WISDOM BINGO

I once had a cohort of students who were particularly adept at crazy wisdom, using it to cope with a professor who drove them batty by using the same phrases and nonverbal communication over and over. To cope with the boredom and annoyance, they created bingo cards with these phrases and habits and passed them out before class to see who would get bingo first. This made me wonder if it were an appropriate use of their time. But they said, "We never paid more attention in class than when playing Professor Bob (not his real name) Bingo," and instead of dreading this class, they looked forward to it and felt they were actually learning more. *That's* crazy wisdom in action.

I have since recommended a version of this when my clients complain about an upcoming visit with family, dreading the predictable comments, digs, conflict, and intoxication. They can use a similar Happy Holiday Bingo game—best kept on a password-protected device—to help them and possibly a partner or sibling who shares a similar perspective to enable them to spend time with family without getting pulled into old, hurtful patterns. Obviously, if the comments are abusive or grossly inappropriate, this isn't the right intervention. But for garden-variety family—or office—annoyances, it can allow you to use crazy wisdom to laugh more than you would otherwise. I recommend a nice box of chocolate as the prize.

Happy Holiday Bingo

Be the first to get 5 in a row!

B	I	N	G	O
Mom comments about my weight	Family unable to agree on restaurant	Dad complains about country club	Sister and I end up doing all the dishes	Sister's kids break something
Dad tells fishing story again	Downward comparison with sis	Mom complains about food	Dad complains about back pain	Can't escape conversation with bro
Mom complains about Aunt Suzie	I pretend that I'm interested in conversation	FREE	Dad lectures about money	Story about awful trip to mountains
Fake photo smile	Parents bicker over where to go	Sister arrives late	Downward comparison with bro	Uncle has too much to drink
Argument over movie to watch	Dad lectures about car maintenance	Kids melt down because of late meal	Mom complains about weather	Argument over family photo

KOANS: RIDDLING CRAZY WISDOM

The most familiar forms of Buddhist crazy wisdom in the West are Zen *koans*, which are riddles or paradoxical anecdotes designed to reveal the inadequacy of the logical mind and stimulate sudden insight. Zen masters consider them a psychiatric intervention to "shock" the disjointed and unenlightened ego into a modicum of stability and sanity.[9] As the mind meditates upon and engages these puzzles, everyday ways of thinking collapse and more enlightened perspectives replace them. They are intended to literally exhaust the logical mind to the point that it finally relaxes, allowing for wisdom and more profound states of mind. More precisely, they are designed to shift one from ordinary, dualistic thinking to non-dualistic thinking and higher states of consciousness. Classic examples include:[10]

- What is the sound of one hand clapping?
- Question: What is the Buddha? Answer: Three pounds of flax.
- If you meet the Buddha on the road, kill him.
- Shut your mouth, close your lips, and say something!
- And, a lesser-known koan: How many bars of chocolate does it take to reach enlightenment?

Zen teachers give their students koans to "blow their minds" out of their habitual way of thinking and open them to the greater truths of what is in the moment. Logic fails to answer the question. Thus you must let your mind ponder, massage, puzzle through it, until the moment when—pop—you get it! It is like a two-by-four that knocks you to the ground—where you roll around, laughing hysterically. Whereas mindfulness is like slow-burning acid on the strings that form your attachments to people, things, and your identity, crazy wisdom cuts through all those strings of attachment at once: with a high-powered Sawzall. Talking about crazy wisdom is one of the surest signs that a person really does not get it. So, I need to stop chatting and invite you to walk my talk!

EXERCISE: SPREADING A LITTLE WISDOM

Now that you are halfway through this book, you should know that you should always keep chocolate handy. Grab the nearest piece of chocolate (or your favorite substitute) and get out of your seat (unless you happen to be in a plane that is taking off or landing). I want you to find a place, function, or recipient for your chocolate that is out of the ordinary. Here are some options to get you thinking:

- Hand it to the nearest stranger or the person who would expect it the least.
- Leave it for someone to find; perhaps attach your own koan or saying: "Truth is in the bean."
- Tape it to the TV remote controller or doorknob.
- Leave it in the hand of a nearby statue or create a boat and let it float in a fountain.
- Put it in a prominent public place with a cryptic note, such as "Tiny pleasures bring the biggest smiles."
- Use it as a bookend, doorstop, or finish on a favorite decoration.

Whatever you do: Do not analyze how best to proceed. Just follow your first thought or impulse. Be playful; feel the magic, energy, and thrill of crazy wisdom. There is no way to do it wrong—except, perhaps, if you are not finding yourself having wild amounts of childlike fun.

WRATHFUL DEITIES AND THE THINGS THAT SCARE YOU

Tibetan Buddhists are also known for their own version of crazy wisdom—it is a more serious form of crazy wisdom. The *Tibetan Book of the Dead* is a book that is read to the deceased soul as it transitions from this life to the next. During this period, one has a rare opportunity to take a shortcut to enlightenment. A series of verses is dedicated to the soul's encounter with wrathful deities, often depicted as blood-drinking dark creatures wearing skull necklaces and holding other grotesque accessories. The closest-looking cousin in the West is the devil, but wrathful deities do not have the same connotation of evil. In marked contrast, they are viewed as part of the cosmic whole and possessing "Buddha nature," possessing a sacred essence or core, if one can look beyond the exterior. Thus, the deceased soul is encouraged to experience these creatures beyond their exterior and embrace them to encounter the Buddha nature that is within them. It is the ultimate lesson on viewing your enemy as your best friend and teacher. The Christian equivalent would be to make friends with the devil: to lose all fear and see how the devil is part of the wisdom of God and necessary for God to do His (or Her) work.

Much of my personal experience with wrathful deities has been on a much smaller scale: spiders. Black widows to be exact. Living in southern California, my garage and yard are crawling with them. I knew they were there but had been able to successfully avoid them for years, until one spring day when my garage door opener was not working right. I went to check and see if the light sensors had been bumped. That is when I met her. The biggest black widow I had ever seen. OK, I had not seen many, but this was bigger than they were in the movies—close to three inches in diameter—just sitting there. She did not move a muscle (if that is the correct anatomic term for what enables them to move their legs). I was certain she was mocking me. I could hear her cartoon voice cackle, "Just try to make me move." I did not know what to do. I have one neighbor who is in the military and the other is a general contractor: as luck would have it, neither was home. What does a single, suburban woman do in this situation? Go to the local hardware store to find a hero—or at least a weapon of localized destruction. Certainly, there must be a spray for such evil. Shocked and dismayed, I discovered they make no such thing. I was on my own.

When I returned home, she was still in the same place, silently smirking. That little three-inch monster had this creature twenty times her size in an absolute panic. I tried to go after her with a shovel; but she outmaneuvered me and got away. I went to bed that night terrified each time I felt the slightest breeze, fearful that she had made her way upstairs.

For the weeks that followed, I was afraid to touch anything in the garage or yard. If I absolutely had to get something, I would engage in a complex series of self-defense maneuvers. First, I would tap the object, checking to see if anything moved. Then I would vigorously shake it. If I saw no movement, I would pull it out and quickly drop it on the floor and then kick it around to make double sure no freeloading spiders had made themselves at home. After carefully checking from all angles, I would finally pick it up and go about my chores. It made putting up the Christmas decorations an unusually laborious task.

One day it hit me. I was actually quite lucky. It had been months since I saw her—the black one—and, apparently, both of us were giving the other enough space to live our lives in peace. It became obvious that she was not going to grow to gargantuan proportions, hunt me down, and murder me in the middle of the night, which the magnitude of my distress seemed to indicate was the underlying fear. I also thought it was curious that God, the universe, ecosystem, or whatever it is that determines the ratio of spiders to humans had made it such that black widows were not overtaking humans like they do in a 1950s thriller. From her grand size, it appeared that she was doing quite well living off the other insects that lived in my garage, who would inhabit the place if she were not there, so perhaps she was helping prevent an even larger pest problem. I noticed how her presence made me mindful of how I moved about my house and garden, paying close attention to my surroundings. It turns out she was helping me to practice what I preached. She was, in a sense, a divine partner—reminding me to stay awake and pay attention, even in my own home. My little wrathful deity had turned into a mini-Buddha. My fear is mostly gone, but my appreciation has grown immensely. The two of us need each other to make each other's lives rich and full of life. The next time I see her I will thank her for touching my life—from a safe distance—with the wild joy of crazy wisdom.

We all have our wrathful deities: the source of evil or ultimate fear. For some, it is their boss, a family member, a political leader, the country next door, another religious group—any rival or identified enemy. Sometimes they see us as their enemy, sometimes not. Often, we are motivated to be our best in our attempt to win the next battle. But it pays to look a little deeper into their eyes to discover who they really are and are not. When you can step back and see the dance, you can see how you two need each other. Each completes the other as the other half. This does not mean that you need to splurge on a red velvet bed for your pet black widow—or an equivalent wrathful deity in your life—but it does mean that you will get to live with a new sense of appreciation, peace, and freedom. Our enemies are only evil if we imagine they are.

MILAREPA: SING OUT THE TRUTH

Milarepa, an eleventh-century Tibetan Buddhist, became known as an enlightened saint who wandered the Himalayas, never settling down.[11] He is best known for his songs, which were sung impromptu in response to his students' questions and critics' remarks or when he would go house to house begging for alms—literally singing for his supper. Similar to koans, his songs are a rare collection of eloquent and profound crazy wisdom, always capturing the play of opposites. For example, consider these, which are adapted for modern non-Buddhist readers: [12]

- To discipline the mind, play like a child.
- Your assumptions are thieves, robbing you of reality in this moment.

- The emptied mind holds everything.
- When your mind is clear, it flows everywhere; although everywhere, not self is found.
- Space is empty. You can say it exists. You can say it does not exist. Both are true.

Music and the arts are favorite venues for crazy wisdom. In modern times, Bradford Keeney, a marriage and family therapist who also studies indigenous healing traditions from around the world, has written extensively about crazy wisdom both generally in terms of spirituality and specifically in terms of Christianity and indigenous healing traditions of the Americas, Africa, Japan, and Australia. His books *Everyday Soul* and *Shamanic Christianity* provide practical guidance for implementing the rare art of crazy wisdom in today's world. One of the ways he encourages readers to learn crazy wisdom is to see life as theater:

> Seeing life as theater helps you take yourself less seriously and develop an actor's appreciation and skill for flexible role assignments. With this flexibility, there is more room for experimentation and improvisation, enabling you to change how you act when the situation calls for your being different.[13]

For most of us hardworking adults, we need permission to be playful, to be creative, to be crazy, to be wise. In our working and educational lives, we are rewarded for conforming, being serious, and following the rules. Play and creative improvisation can get us in trouble at times. That may still be the case at work or school, but do not bring those rules home with you to your personal and family life. I hope that the air traffic controllers, bankers, and surgeons in my life do not get overly creative or playful with their work, but if their personal lives are to be filled with extraordinary happiness, they must be different at home. The trick is to see work roles as theatrical roles we "play" at work (yes, it seems to be a double paradox), but we are free to be someone else at home.

If acting is not your thing, maybe dance, music, or art is a better way of thinking about crazy wisdom. I love to dance. So, I find it helpful to ask myself: How am I dancing with this person or situation? What is our rhythm? Are we in sync? Are we even dancing the same dance? Are we having fun? These questions help me find better ways of relating.

I once worked with a couple who said they almost never laughed together. They claimed it was like this from the beginning, but I was suspicious that cupid could have denied them! They had fallen out of love and were not sure how to get the feeling back. Therefore, this couple's therapy consisted primarily of learning to play rather than to communicate better about problems because, in fact, they communicated well. Brad Keeney has a saying: Play is hard work.[14] But I never knew it could be as hard as it was for this couple.

I began by asking them to create a mini-adventure or playtime during their Saturday out doing errands: stop at the park and play on the swings, play a "road game" you used on family trips as a child, get a favorite childhood treat and eat it like you did as a child—drips and all. They could not do it. We tried practical jokes—no go either. Favorite comedies and games—not helpful. After many tries and perhaps their feeling guilty that they had not tried anything else, we found it: playing with food. During dinnertime, we made it a family game to communicate something about the day with the "food of the night": mashed potatoes, green beans, or a tortilla. There was laughter—more than they ever remember having had. Not surprisingly, their affection for each other soon trickled back—and they finally learned to play in other areas of their life, even without their kids present.

IF YOU MEET THE BUDDHA . . .

There is a famous Buddhist koan: If you meet the Buddha on the road, kill him.[15] It is quite odd if you consider the fact that Buddhists are strict with their teachings of nonviolence. They would never head to a hardware store for bug spray. So, what is going on here? Essentially, this koan teaches a critical crazy wisdom lesson that getting attached to even the greatest teachings or teacher is a problem.

Often, we become attached to teachings, religion, spiritual teachers, or the spiritual path more generally in a way that it is detrimental to our growth. There is a paradoxical effect where what starts out opening our minds actually results in shutting them down. This is common in all religions, whether traditional or New Age. People's level of attachment to their spiritual path is revealed in how easily offended they are when others disagree with their views. In our culture, we see it most clearly in the extreme forms of cults, especially those that have involved the dramatic deaths of its members. We see it more subtly around the family table when tempers flare over the correct interpretation of God's Word. In both cases, what should be a liberating, joy-filled teaching turns into a source of darkness and division.

The point of this koan is to remind us not to take even the deepest truth too seriously—because that too will become your prison. The ability to laugh at the limitations and rigid formalities of one's practice and beliefs is a sign of being open to what is ultimately greater, wiser, and more infinite than the human mind can comprehend. If you do not find yourself laughing with God or Buddha, you may not have met yet. But if you keep showing up at the playground, I am sure you will eventually be introduced.

THE DISCIPLINE OF CRAZY WISDOM

Crazy wisdom is serious business. It is not the nonsense of escapism or mindless ignorance—far from it. Crazy wisdom is a sacred art. From the outside, it may be hard to tell the difference. But for the practitioner, there is a big difference. How can you tell?

- **Crazy Wisdom Opens the Heart:** The quickest way to tell random silliness from crazy wisdom is that the latter is always fueled by love, kindness, and a gentle heart. It is not joking or teasing that carries a dark undertone or hurtful message. Instead, it opens and softens the heart. What was once an enemy becomes a friend; what was once rejected is embraced; what was once feared is loved.
- **Crazy Wisdom Liberates:** You will know you have tripped over crazy wisdom because you will feel freed from your box— often it is a box you did not even know you were in. You feel the shackles drop and cannot restrain yourself from dancing. When you make friends with the black widow in your garage or the enemy at the office, all of a sudden the weight of those fears and troubles are lifted from your shoulder. It feels great.
- **Crazy Wisdom Opens the Mind:** When the lightning of crazy wisdom strikes, it blows your mind. What you once took

as unshakable truth lies in ruins on the floor—and, after the shock wears off, you are thankful. One more illusion is shattered, allowing truth to stream through. Like the night I discovered that a European restaurant did not have chocolate—an illusion shattered to make way for real life, real friendships, and new adventures.

- **Crazy Wisdom Frees the Soul:** The soul craves crazy wisdom. It dances upon the shattered illusions on the floor, and for a moment, you are connected to the larger intelligence that organizes the universe. The Divine Comedy reveals itself, and all is OK in the world. The laughter is fueled by a deeper joy of knowing everything is and will forever be OK.
- **Crazy Wisdom Makes Friends:** You will also know when you have stumbled upon crazy wisdom because it invites others in and brings people together. The zaniness opens hearts so that even sworn enemies lay down their weapons and play.

And scientists inform us that crazy wisdom is one of two forms of humor—self-enhancing humor—that enables us to weather difficulty and increases our sense of overall well-being.

TICKLING THE BUDDHA'S BELLY

So how do you learn the art of crazy wisdom? Find a trouble, a struggle, an enemy, a boredom, and learn how to play with it. That is what makes it a discipline. In the moment when you most want to be angry, hurt, vengeful, or mean, you must pause and change direction. In your most vulnerable moment, you choose to open up rather than protect yourself. When it makes no sense to leap, you decide to trust anyway and you jump. To get you started, let's end with some refreshing ways to get your daily dose of laughter:

Joke-a-Day: Sign up to have some fun delivered to your inbox each morning or subscribe to or visit sites with humor for just about everyone:

- http://www.laughfactory.com/jokes/joke-of-the-day
- http://www.jokesoftheday.net
- http://www.funny-jokes-quotes.com

Create Your Own Mad Libs: Find the dreariest thing you had to read today—a phone bill, work email, tax form, news article. Then take a black marker and cross out every fifth word for the first paragraph or two. Then without having him or her see the full text, ask a friend to replace the words, replacing verbs with another verb; nouns with nouns, and so on. Then read the mad lib aloud for you both to enjoy.

Crazy Wisdom First-Aid Kit: Brad Keeney recommends creating a crazy wisdom first-aid kit or medicine bag.[16] The kit should contain:

- A sacred feather
- A miniature toy animal, ideally of an animal that you find humorous
- A stack of cards with your favorite crazy-wisdom quotes, either your own or taken from a master of the art.

Over the years, I have collected a list of random sayings from various posts and emails sent to me by friends, some of which emerged from our various life experiences (I'll let you guess which ones):

- Some days you are the bug; some days you are the windshield.
- Complex problems have simple, easy-to-understand wrong answers.
- It may be that your sole purpose in life is simply to serve as a warning to others.
- A closed mouth gathers no foot.
- Never test the depth of the water with both feet.
- Good judgment comes from bad experience, and a lot of that comes from bad judgment.
- Before you criticize someone, you should walk a mile in their shoes. That way, when you criticize them, you are a mile away and you have their shoes.
- Warning: Dates on calendar are closer than they appear.
- If at first you don't succeed, skydiving is not for you. If at first you *do* succeed, try not to look too astonished.
- The quickest way to double your money is to fold it in half and put it back in your pocket.
- If it isn't broken, take it apart, lose a few pieces, and it soon will be.
- Duct tape is like the force; it has a light side and a dark side, and it holds the universe together.

- Generally speaking, you aren't learning much when your mouth is moving.
- Experience is something you don't get until just after you need it.
- It is impossible to make anything foolproof because fools are so ingenious.
- After all is said and done, a hell of a lot more is said than done.
- Never argue with an idiot; listeners may not notice the difference.
- First law of laboratory work: Hot glass looks exactly the same as cold glass.
- The man who invented the eraser had the human race pretty well sized up.
- Eat a live toad the first thing in the morning and nothing worse will happen to you the rest of the day.

Put the feather, toy animal, and cards with your favorite quotes in a box or bag labeled "crazy wisdom emergency kit." The next time you have one of those overly somber days where you need an extra dose of crazy wisdom, pull out your box. Grab the feather and tickle your little animal and read through your stack of quotes. It's a serious form of healing over-seriousness.

• 7 •

Fierce Compassion

Opening Your Heart to Milk, White, and Dark

I need to add the ending to my crazy wisdom chocolate adventure in Germany. After a night of virtual chocolate, the next morning when I opened my door I found a box of fine Belgian chocolates from Kordula, one of the therapists in the class. Her name literally means "heart" in Latin. Somehow that night or early that morning, she found a place that sold fine chocolates. I never asked, but it may have been the *Tankstelle* after all. No matter the source, when I saw the box my heart melted—to be shown such kindness from a person I had known for only a few days. As a teacher, I know it is foolish to ever expect to be shown true appreciation until long after the educational event is over—it is not until a student takes a teacher's lesson and tries to apply it in the real world that the student knows how valuable the lesson was or was not. The timing of her gift made it especially meaningful to me.

Kordula's kindness—and similar acts of a generous heart—are the key that unlocks the full force of both mindfulness and crazy wisdom and carries you on your way to extraordinary happiness. Without an open heart, happiness is impossible to achieve. This may sound obvious, but if you take a look around, it is not readily apparent in the world today or even in our own backyards: wars, lawsuits, abused children, hostile words with loved ones. We are most likely to open our hearts to a select few: our favorite family members and closest friends. Ironically, on a bad day, these are the very people we are most likely to hurt and abuse. Sometimes we are moved to conduct random acts of kindness with a stranger: buying lunch for a homeless person; helping an elderly lady with her groceries; purchasing holiday gifts for children whose family cannot. The Buddhists teach us that showing compassion for our

113

loved ones and select others is only a warm-up exercise—practice for the much more challenging art of fierce compassion, which is the secret to extraordinary happiness.

BUDDHIST VIEW OF COMPASSION

The heart of Buddhist teachings is compassion.[1] You cannot understand any of the other teachings without understanding how this force fuels all Buddhist practices. Without compassion, mindfulness is nothing more than mind control. Without compassion, crazy wisdom is nothing more than a practical joke. Without compassion, even the Buddhist practice of vegetarianism is just another fad diet.

So, what is the Buddhist definition of compassion? The most common translation is *loving-kindness*: a willingness to step outside of yourself in order to understand another, and at times yourself, *through your heart*, inspiring loving and kind actions and words. These teachings are similar to the Christian teachings based on the life of Jesus Christ. Whereas Christianity teaches compassion through the relatively indirect means of parables, the Buddhists use a disciplined approach to develop compassion consciously and deliberately.

In Tibetan monasteries, monks and nuns spend the first year practicing loving-kindness meditation and practicing compassion through traditions such as vegetarianism. Buddhists practice vegetarianism not because it is healthy for the physical heart but rather the emotional heart: it teaches compassion for living creatures. It is an ever-present reminder of the sanctity of all sentient life, from that of a small ant to a great elephant. Killing a black widow, which I admittedly have successfully done once, is not consistent with Buddhist teachings. For the Buddhists, a compassionate heart is cultivated through discipline and regular daily practice that I have not seen in any other community.

LOVING-KINDNESS MEDITATION

The most common form of compassion meditation is loving-kindness or *metta* (from Pali) meditation.[2] Originating from Tibetan and East Asian Mahayana traditions, loving-kindness meditation involves more visualization than traditional mindfulness practices—and you get to silently use language, more enjoyable for some. In this meditation, you send positive, loving energy and intentions to a variety of people, including loved ones, acquaintances, oneself, and "enemies," persons with whom one has a strained or difficult relationship. Compared with mindfulness, I find this one always lifts my mood and brings a smile.

COMPASSION MEDITATION NO. 1: LOVING-KINDNESS MEDITATION

You can use this meditation guide or the guided meditation at www.mindfulness forchoclateloves.com.

Acquaintance, Stranger, or Neutral Other

Call to mind someone you have seen recently, but do not know very well personally, such as a person on a bus/train or a clerk at a store. Now send this person well wishes.

- May you feel great happiness and joy.
- May you be free from physical pain, harm, and illness.
- May you live with a sense of ease and freedom.
- May you be happy, healthy, and at peace.

Significant Other

Call to mind someone you love. For now, just choose one person; you can go back and send wishes to others later. Now send this person well wishes.

- May you feel great happiness and joy.
- May you be free from physical pain, harm, and illness.
- May you live with a sense of ease and freedom.
- May you be happy, healthy, and at peace.

Difficult Other

Call to mind someone with whom you have a difficult relationship right now; perhaps he or she has harmed you in some way or you cannot find a way past a disagreement. For a moment, put those thoughts aside and try to see him or her as a person who also suffers, and send this person well wishes.

- May you feel great happiness and joy.
- May you be free from physical pain, harm, and illness.
- May you live with a sense of ease and freedom.
- May you be happy, healthy, and at peace.

Self

Finally, you are going to send well wishes to yourself.

• May you feel great happiness and joy.
• May you be free from physical pain, harm, and illness.
• May you live with a sense of ease and freedom.
• May you be happy, healthy, and at peace.

Reflection

• Notice how you are feeling right now.
• Notice the differences in sending positive intentions to each person.

FIERCE COMPASSION

In certain forms of Buddhism, there is a second form of compassion: fierce compassion, which has two forms. First, more traditionally, it is loving that which you cannot love, often an enemy, one who stands for all you detest, one who has tried to hurt you and those you love. That takes fierce compassion. The night I stared death in the face so that I could keep my heart open to my dying husky Tara, I practiced fierce compassion. The day I ceased my war with the black widow, I practiced fierce compassion. When the Dalai Lama speaks with sincere respect for China, he is practicing fierce compassion. As Eleanor Roosevelt said, "You must do the thing you cannot do." When that means to love what you cannot love, you are practicing fierce compassion.

The other form of fierce compassion is perhaps similar to what we know as "tough love." Often, I hear this term used to refer to a heartless type of parenting, but that is not the actual meaning. Loving our children, students, partners, friends, and coworkers fiercely means that there are times when we must make a difficult decision that may not be popular but is necessary either for the other's well-being or our own. In most cases, these moments involve saying "no" to what the other wants: "No, I can't give you that"; "No, I won't give you that"; "No, I cannot do that for you."

As a family therapist, one of the most concerning trends I see in today's families is parents who are unwilling to do the difficult task of saying no to their children's inappropriate demands. Similarly, as a couples therapist, I often hear that one person—most often the female partner in a heterosexual relationship—"falls out of love" after years of not standing up for herself because it was easier to ignore her needs than assert them. Similarly, many men report that they decide to not state their true thoughts to keep the peace, which eventually leads to them "losing it" verbally or physically. In such situations, fierce compassion involves learning how to set such boundaries with sincere love for the other. Waiting until you finally get angry and explode upon or give up on others unexpectedly is rarely effective.

THE SCIENCE OF COMPASSION

Some people are motivated to be compassionate because it seems like the "right" thing to do. Or it just comes naturally. But for those who need some convincing, scientists have been studying the effects of compassion meditation, which you now know is distinct from mindfulness. In a systematic review of twenty studies on loving-kindness meditation with persons experiencing psychological distress, U.K. researchers found improvements in five areas of functioning:

- Less negative and more positive affect/mood
- Reduced psychological distress
- Increased positive thinking
- Improved interpersonal relations
- Enhanced empathic accuracy (ability to read the emotions of others)[3]

Similarly, Harvard professor Dr. Christina Luberto led an international team of researchers to conduct a review and meta-analysis of the effectiveness of compassion meditation.[4] They also found significant results for improvements in positive emotions, empathy, and behaviors, even when compassion meditation was compared with other forms of intervention, attributing these improvements to both psychosocial and neurobiological changes.

Researchers have also explored whether practicing meditations designed to increase compassion actually work. In one study, more than one hundred graduate counseling students, who tend to have higher-than-average levels of compassion, learned loving-kindness meditation in a six-week course.[5] At the end of the class, there was a significant increase in their levels of compassion and their ability to consider others' perspectives, with those who practiced more having significantly improved perspective taking. Findings from a study at Ohio University provided additional evidence that compassion meditation's primary effect is on empathy. David Weibel and colleagues conducted a randomized clinical trial that examined the effectiveness of loving-kindness meditation on compassion and anxiety.[6] They found that after the four-week meditation class, participants significantly increased in their compassion for others and themselves, but their anxiety levels did not change.

In reviewing the research findings, researchers have proposed a model for understanding how compassion meditation changes a person's response to suffering.[7] They suggest that regular practice of compassion meditation results in the following:

1. Increasing empathic responses when witnessing the suffering of others
2. Decreasing avoidance of suffering and painful stimuli
3. Increasing a compassionate response to the suffering of others

If none of this convinced you to try compassion meditation, would weight loss and slowing the aging process stimulate your interest? British researchers found that participants who practiced mindfulness with loving-kindness meditation lost more weight over one year than either the mindfulness-only group or the control group at the end of one year.[8] Apparently, compassion meditation reduces the stress that relates to weight management, but I can't figure out how researchers decided to investigate such a possibility.

Equally surprising, researchers at Massachusetts General Hospital measured the telomere length—a part of cells that affects how we age, with shorter length a marker of accelerated aging—of participants who practice loving-kindness meditation and those who do not. Compassion meditation practitioners had significantly longer telomere length (slower aging) than those who did not; this was especially true for women.[9] Thus these researchers identified two unexpected, self-serving, and hard-to-beat benefits to cultivating kindness for others.

COMPASSION AND MINDFULNESS MEDITATIONS: HEAD-TO-HEAD

Several teams of researchers have been curious as to whether mindfulness and compassion meditations have similar or different effects on practitioners, so they tested them head-to-head. In one study, researchers examined the difference between persons practicing loving-kindness versus mindfulness meditation.[10] While both showed an increase in positive mood, those practicing compassion meditation had a higher "dose" response than those practicing mindfulness, meaning the more they practice the greater the benefits. Similarly, a group of British researchers identified which meditation benefited particular depressive symptoms more. They found that depressed patients with a tendency for brooding—replaying negative thoughts repeatedly in their heads—responded better to mindfulness meditation, whereas those depressed patients who did little brooding responded better to loving-kindness meditation.[11] This finding indicates that the "refocusing" aspect of mindfulness may directly help brooding types interrupt their ruminating thoughts. In contrast, compassion meditation may help those who overfocus on the negative reconnect with more positive thoughts and memories.

Curious about physiological effects, a team of researchers in Hong Kong decided to use magnetic resonance imaging (MRI) to see if any brain differences could be detected between the two forms of meditation.[12] They found that mindfulness improved performance on tasks requiring focus and attention; compassion meditation didn't affect performance on these cognitive tasks. However, when compassion meditation practitioners viewed sad faces, their processing involved emotional regulation and separating their feelings from the subjects, whereas mindfulness practitioners' responses were more related to cognitive processing. Thus, different types of meditations have measurably different effects on the brain, with mindfulness appearing to improve cognitive function and compassion enhancing emotional functioning.

FIERCE COMPASSION: BEYOND FALLING IN LOVE

As a marriage and family therapist, I regularly have people come to my office talking about love: how they had it and lost it; how they love their children but do not know how to help manage their behaviors or moods; how they love their spouses but are frustrated and angry with their words and actions; how they are in love with another person but are afraid to leave their current partner. At its heart, the solution for all involves learning to love *fiercely*.

Falling in love is easy. In most cases, it seems that you do not have a choice. There is little effort or thought, whether you are falling in love with the man or woman of your dreams or the first sight of your child or grandchild. When love is fresh, it is easy to be compassionate and kind. It is hard to be any other way. That is why the Dalai Lama says practicing compassion with those you love and who love you back is not the truest way to cultivate compassion: you have a good business deal going on, agreeing to return kindness with kindness. But once the chemistry settles down, which according to scientists generally does between eighteen and twenty-four months into romantic partnerships, that is when the real loving begins. That is when you move from loving because you are driven by the chemistry, freshness, and excitement, to making a choice to act and speak with love and kindness each day. For parents, this may happen around two and then again at twelve—or at any time your child has decided to explore the full potential of the word "no" in relation to you.

In these moments, courage enters the picture. To love fully day to day, you must choose to love not only when the beloved reciprocates, but also when the "exchange rate" is not so good. Your partner says something cruel or your child disobeys, and you want to defend yourself, strike back, shut down, or run away. But this is precisely the moment when you must have the courage to love. You must find a way to keep your heart open in the moment when it is most vulnerable, fearful, and hurt. I believe this is the truest of loves, and it is the rarest because few have learned how to muster the courage.

Although fierce compassion does not mean you fight fire with fire, it also does not mean you lie down like a doormat and blindly accept cruelty from others. That would be too easy. Appeasing others is a common yet ultimately fear-based coping style that simply involves allowing yourself to suffer to avoid the anger of others. In most world cultures, women have historically been expected to put their needs aside for men and children to keep societal and familial peace and stability. In the end, this does not benefit them or their relationships (but it does make getting through a difficult meal at a restaurant less embarrassing).

So, what does fierce compassion look like? It means having compassion for the other and self at the same time, even when you are scared, angry, hurt, or otherwise wanting to attack or flee. It involves setting boundaries with kindness, love, and respect. If you cannot do it in a difficult moment, you wait until you can. It is easy to be a bulldozer or the one who gets bulldozed over, but fierce compassion is standing between the two saying, "This must end; I see the suffering that drove both of us to this, but I refuse to let it continue." I cannot promise that everyone will appreciate your efforts; that is precisely why it takes courage to love fiercely. You are not guaranteed that your kindness will be returned with kindness. But you will come to find that loving fiercely is the only way to love if you want to live a life of extraordinary happiness.

ARE YOU READY TO LOVE?

Just as Buddhists approach happiness as a life skill, they approach love as a *skill* that can be consciously cultivated. Unfortunately, in the West, we approach happiness and love as something that involves luck, chemistry, or other external circumstances, only partially under our conscious control. However, Western science supports the Buddhist approach more than the culture's popular notions. The question is: are you willing to let go of the Western armchair version of love—the idea that love should come naturally and easily—and start practicing the Buddhist art of fierce compassion? When I say practice, I mean *practice*—like learning a new sport or musical instrument. Each day requires concentrated effort on learning this skill. When you finally become ready, the world is ready and eager to receive your open heart.

THE FOUR RELATIONSHIPS

There are four types of relationships that allow you to readily cultivate compassion. The first three are used in classic Buddhist teachings on cultivating compassion: (1) relationship with stranger, (2) relationship with friend/loved one, and (3) relationship with enemy. The last one I add, as do other Western Buddhist teachers, because it is an especially problematic relationship in the West: (4) the relationship you have with yourself.

In my practice as a therapist, I have noticed some people need to first learn how to love others before they can be kind to themselves. Others need to start to learn how to have compassion for themselves before they can cultivate it for others. In either case, as you learn to have more compassion for yourself, you have more compassion for others. The more compassion you have for others, the better able you are to love and accept who you are. These two forms of compassion mutually reinforce each other.

It is impossible to condemn and hate others without doing the same to yourself on some level. Once this understanding sinks into your being, compassion becomes contagious. You see the fear and vulnerability that underlies all hatred and unkindness in this world. You have the courage to stand in front of bulldozers, return a cruel remark with wisdom, and extend kindness to—or at least not attack—those you fear. You have the courage because it is the only thing that makes sense when you understand the true nature of the heart.

LEARNING FIERCE COMPASSION FROM STRANGERS

Although contrary to what you may see walking down an average street on any given day, strangers really are the easiest place to start cultivating compassion. Why? There is virtually no risk because you have no history with them and likely never will. If you are rejected or they don't respond in kind, it won't hurt you the same way as someone you care about. They may respond in a friendly way; they may respond in a hostile way; they may not respond at all. You should hope for all of these responses because they give you a small taste of how the more regular characters in your life will respond, allowing you to hone your heart skills.

When you think of strangers, think outside the box. Strangers, by definition, are not only those you do not know personally, but also those who are different from yourself. People can be different in terms of gender, age, race, ethnicity, culture, income, social class, personality, values, religion, occupation, family life, social life, and lifestyle. In learning compassion, it is also helpful to include all living things—plants, insects, spiders, wild animals, sea creatures—all beings that we can cause to suffer. They have much to teach us also.

So where do you start? I think the easiest place to begin is with a meditation I learned at a training with Jack Kornfield many years ago. I have since used variations of this life review meditation to teach therapy students how to generate compassion for their clients, classmates, and partners.

COMPASSION MEDITATION NO. 2: A DAY-IN-THE-LIFE MEDITATION

There are a few ways to do this meditation. First, if possible, find a person who is willing to do the exercise with you, perhaps a friend or family member. Sit across from one another and look into each other's eyes as you follow along with the meditation. This is a very intense and intimate exercise, so allow yourself and the other person to look away whenever necessary to be comfortable, remembering that this is not a staring contest. You are practicing kindness, so do not judge yourself or the other person during this process. Keep your heart open to where each of you is at the present moment. Alternatively, you can look at yourself in a mirror or at a picture of someone you know or don't know. Once you have identified a person, you can follow along with this written guide or listen to the meditation at www.mindfulnessforchocolatelovers.com.

Gaze at the Other

Begin by looking into the eyes of the other. What do you feel? How are you feeling in this moment? Just take a moment to get acquainted with her eyes.

Today

Imagine the possibilities of this person's day up to this point:

- *Challenges:* What type of challenges could this day have possibly included? Perhaps she had difficulty getting up, received a stressful call, or found a stain on the shirt she intended to wear. Perhaps she had an argument with a loved one or friend. Perhaps she received some bad news, hit traffic, or lost her keys. Just imagine for a moment all the little struggles that this person may have encountered this morning. Open your heart to these little sufferings.
- *Excitements:* Now reflect on other aspects of her morning. Perhaps she woke up excited about the day—feeling hopeful and alive. Perhaps she had a moment to savor the perfect cup of coffee, tea with a touch of honey, the spray from a piece of fruit, sunlight streaming through the kitchen window, cool air on her face during a morning jog, or hot water on her back as she stepped into the shower. Share in the joy of a good morning kiss, the generosity of a kind word from someone she loves, or a phone call with good news. Spend a few moments imagining and savoring the joys of the morning.

Current Life Situation

Struggles: Imagine what burdens this person may be carrying with her at this time in her life. Perhaps there are problems at work, struggles with loved ones, concerns about her health, worries about finances. Wonder if there are burdens that no one else knows about or shares. Touch that loneliness.

Joys: Now, imagine the small victories, joys, and pleasures that may be happening in this person's life right now. Perhaps she has recently experienced a great success at work; perhaps she has recently had a friend come through when she needed this person most; perhaps her child has hit a new milestone; perhaps one of her greatest life dreams has finally come true. See the light and joy in her eyes; hear her laughter; see the light radiate from her whole being. Share in this moment; drink it in with her. Find joy in her joy.

Birth and Childhood

Birth: Now, go back and imagine the day this person was born. Wonder what was going through her parents' minds. Were they excited, fearful, worried, confident? Were the parents together or was the mother alone? Was this child a surprise or the fulfillment of a long-awaited dream? Imagine the moment that the mother first saw and held this child. Feel a love that burns so brightly she does not feel her own pain. Imagine the first time the father held his child; feel his delight, pride, and joy.

Childhood Joys: Imagine as the child grew up, her first taste of ice cream—perhaps it was chocolate. See the child's face beaming with excitement at this amazing experience. Imagine the excitement of kicking a soccer ball, playing on a swing, dancing to a nursery rhyme, giggling with a puppy, listening to a bedtime story. Feel the joys of childhood.

Childhood Struggles: Now turn your attention to the struggles of childhood. The first time she heard the word "no" when she really, really wanted something. The cruel words from kids on the playground, telling her how she was ugly, unwanted, or not good enough. Remember the first big fall, bloody knees and chin; perhaps she was all alone and not sure what to do. Imagine the first big fight with her parents, when she was not sure if she was truly loved anymore. Embrace this child's hurts and share your warmth and comfort with this child.

End of Life

Life Review: Fast forward to the end of this person's life. Imagine her on her deathbed. Wonder who—if anyone—is by her side. Walk with her as she reviews her life: the good times, the hard times, her failures, her successes, the joy and sorrow. Are her regrets greater than her sense of peace? Is she able to finally open up to forgive those who have hurt her, make peace with her family, make peace with herself? Imagine her family and friends and the loss they will soon be feeling.

Last Moments: Look into this person's eyes in her last moments. Think about all the ways her life has made a difference in this world, even in the smallest of ways. Imagine both the joy and pain she brought to this world. Appreciate this person on behalf of all those whose lives she has blessed; imagine forgiveness for this person on behalf of all those she has hurt. Find the courage to lovingly be with this person at the moment of her last breath.

If you still have dry eyes, you need to repeat this exercise until they leak. You will always be moved when you get a glimpse of the fullness and miraculousness of human life. Each person has a story that includes joys and pain, and often this pain is kept hidden for fear of how others might react. After doing this meditation, try to bring to your mind the billions of people who are alive today, and how each one has such a story. If you can imagine that, then think of all the people who have ever walked this planet. That is a lot of suffering and a lot of joy to behold. The more you can keep this image in mind, the easier it will be to summon fierce compassion in your life.

The task now is to transfer the insight from the Day-in-the-Life Meditation to your everyday life. For this, we will draw from a Jewish writer, Martin Buber. Buber proposed that there were two ways of relating to the world: I-It and I-Thou relationships.[13] Of necessity, we must interact with others as I-Its in most of our interactions, meaning we interact based on our roles, such as parent–child, husband–wife, employer–employee, friend–friend, service worker–customer, doctor–patient, and teacher–student. In these situations, the other is an It, an object, in our awareness with whom we interact. We interact based on our social roles to get things done and keep our society running.

In contrast, in I-Thou relationships, we fully acknowledge the other as a unique being with his or her unique experiences, feelings, and meanings. In this last meditation, you experienced the other person as a Thou. Hopefully, when you look at relationships with friends and family you can think of moments when the other person was a Thou: when you fully experienced their unique personhood. Words may or may not have been exchanged, but somehow you were able to open your heart and mind to the other, making space to hear and receive their thoughts and feelings. When you are the recipient of such understanding, you know that in that moment you are not alone on the planet and never will be fully alone again. I-Thou moments are when soul touches soul. With exception of individuals like Mother Teresa, we cannot spend every waking moment in I-Thou connection with others. However, we can increase the frequency and duration of such moments.

Surprisingly, one of the easiest places to cultivate I-Thou moments is with strangers. Often, those closest to you do not want to share in the moment—they have more to risk than a total stranger who will never see you again. Your loved ones have to face you again—

after such vulnerability. And, of course, your enemies usually do not want to play this game. In contrast, strangers are often more open to a quick moment of being touched, of being real.

For example, the other day, I was at a coffee house very early on a Sunday morning. Realizing that the workers had to be there much earlier than myself to make my cup of tea, I playfully commented to the woman taking my order, "No one should be up at this ungodly hour on a Sunday, but I really appreciate you being here to provide me with my morning caffeine." Soon, the other worker joined in, and we were swapping some very creative alarm clock strategies and laughing. I left with a smile on my face, feeling meaningfully connected to these would-be strangers. I am fairly sure our conversation brightened their day, and hopefully they felt more appreciated for their efforts in serving the world as they do. I encourage you to practice this exercise for a couple of weeks and see if it does not make a difference in your life.

EXERCISE: I-THOU EXPERIMENTS: PART I

First Week: I-Thou with Strangers

Over the next week, look for opportunities to invite I-Thou moments with strangers. The key to success is to not try *too* hard. Although such connection is meaningful, these moments don't have to be earthshaking or deep, soul-searching conversations, especially with total strangers—that would be creepy. Instead, whenever you have a chance to interact with strangers, try to find a way to honor and respect their humanity by considering potential sufferings or joys. Remind yourself of how this person's mother or best friend likely views him, and then ask yourself questions such as these to consider how to see the person as a *Thou* rather than an *It*: How might this person be feeling today? What are the challenges this person may be experiencing right now? How might I bring a little light to his day? How could I bring out this person's beauty and goodness with my words or actions? How might I connect with the best part of him for even the briefest moment?

Some Ways to Make I-Thou Connection

- Use compliments to acknowledge a specific thing about the stranger (e.g., "You make that look easy.").
- Show empathy for the person's potential suffering (e.g., "I hope you get a chance to get out this weekend and have some fun, too.").
- Be appreciative of the person's help and kindness (e.g., "Thank you for helping me find the blue one; it will make my son's birthday.").

- Be curious about who this person is, how he is feeling, or what he is doing (e.g., "Where did you learn to do . . .").

Ordering coffee or a meal, checking out at the grocery store, getting into an elevator, or standing in line are all times and places where you can practice encountering the Thou in others. When I assign this task to my students, someone always asks, but what if the person does not reciprocate or does not want to talk? Then, have compassion for that, too. Although not everyone I have met responds to me with as much warmth, I have never met anyone who did not appreciate being treated this way—except for passport control officers, who I believe are forbidden by law to smile in most countries.

As you learn to master the art of engaging strangers as a Thou, you will soon find that kind people are almost everywhere you go. The world becomes a much friendlier place.

LEARNING FIERCE COMPASSION FROM LOVED ONES AND FRIENDS

One would think that it would be easiest to practice fierce compassion with friends and loved ones. But that is not the case. Why? I think the answer is twofold. First, we get caught up in how their behavior and words affect us, making it hard to welcome all of who and what they are. If someone we love is unhappy, angry, ill, or having a meltdown or midlife crisis, it affects us—we may have to give up dinner plans, sacrifice something we want, or move across the country. We may feel judged as not enough or that we do not matter to the one we love. We may be asked to change, which is rarely a welcomed message. Second, our loved ones might have the same fears.

How do our friends and loved ones teach us fierce compassion? More than anyone else, we get to know them fully—in all their humanity, both their greatness and weakness. No one can be perfect. We all have flaws, imperfections, frailties, or at least parts of ourselves that at least one other person on the planet will find annoying. In most relationships, we learn to hide the parts of ourselves that the other does not welcome. Each of us subtly—or not so subtly—sends cues to the other through our anger, a look in our eyes, or a long-held resentment about the behaviors we reject in the other. So, we hobble about like half-finished puzzles, each trying to make the other person feel more comfortable. But it is hard to be comfortable when only part of you is there.

The easiest person to learn how to love fiercely is not your parents (but you knew that), your spouse, or your child, but your best friends. Perhaps because their lives are linked voluntarily to us and it is easier to get out, it is easier to take the risk to show yourself fully to a friend, and in return, accept a friend fully in turn. You can share your deep-held secret—the one that significant others would likely judge because they may experience some of the fallout—with a true friend and know that your friend will listen long enough to understand why you did what you did. In the end, we all make the best decision we can in any given moment with the information we have. In that moment, it was the best we could do, and sometimes we are weaker than others. True friends find the courage to listen and open their hearts to our ugliest parts, the parts we reject in ourselves. When you love another after seeing all of who that person is—the good, the bad, and the parts you find ugly—you are practicing fierce compassion, also known as true love.

I-THOU EXPERIMENTS: PART II

Week Two: Friends and Loved Ones

For the second week, try to do this with loved ones. Surprisingly, it is often more difficult to shift to an I-Thou connection with someone we know well because the stakes of being fully present are higher.

LEARNING FIERCE COMPASSION FROM ENEMIES

I will not lie to you. This is where it gets hard. This is also where fierce compassion is truly learned. In the arms of the enemy, the one who you believe is wrong, the one who has hurt you or someone you love. Your ego tells you that this person should suffer because of what he or she has done or failed to do. This is the one who will teach you fierce compassion; this is the one who will teach you true love. No one else really can.

Tibetan Buddhists have a unique and special compassion meditation called *tonglen*.[14] From all traditions, this meditation stands out as the one that teaches fierce compassion most directly and simply. Unlike any meditation I have heard of, in this meditation, you breathe *in* the suffering of others and breathe *out* light, blessings, and love. It takes courage to be willing to take in another's pain and suffering. If you dare to do so, you will find each breath makes your heart stronger and fiercer—fierce enough to love your enemy.

Tonglen shatters our fear of darkness, pain, and suffering. It teaches us that, when we open our hearts, we can transform the darkness of this world. I have worked with hundreds of people who have been the victims of sexual abuse: children, women, and men. Undoubtedly, sexual abuse is one of the most horrific things that can happen to a person. It is also one of the most treatable conditions that I see as a therapist. Healing is *always* possible. In my first meeting with people who want to heal from sexual abuse, the most important thing I do is look in their eyes and say, "Life will be normal again. You can heal from this—your child can heal from this."

What I don't reveal is what it requires of me. I have to join them in their painful nightmare. I have to become fully present to the horror they endured. I enter their world, take their hand, and lead them back to safety and healing. It's never easy but always worth it. I've done it hundreds of times and will do so any time I have the honor to help another in this way. Like Virgil in Dante's *Inferno*, I believe I have become a skilled guide through and out of hell.

Tonglen and practices like it have helped me to open my heart to suffering so that I can see it, choose to embrace it, and use the transformational power of the heart to heal it. My courage to be a witness to the horror of a person's abuse gives them the courage to see it, acknowledge it, and feel it, and in doing so, the suffering dissipates like rain puddles that evaporate when the sun finally emerges after a storm. The road is usually quite difficult, but healing is assured if we stay the path. Fierce compassion makes us invincible, even when confronted with unimaginable darkness.

COMPASSION MEDITATION NO. 3: STRANGER, FRIEND, AND ENEMY

You can use the guided meditation at www.mindfulnessforchocolatelovers.com or use this meditation guide.

Stranger or Acquaintance

Bring to mind someone you do not know well. A stranger, an acquaintance, someone you see often but do not know much about, including her name. Imagine this person before you in your mind's eye. As you imagine this person, let her suffering come to mind. You can imagine the suffering that all humans experience: illness and physical discomfort; losing a loved one; rejection from those they hope to impress; failing at a task they worked hard to achieve; not having enough money, time, or resources to fulfill their desires.

Inhale Suffering

Imagine breathing in the darkness, the weight, the stickiness of her suffering and pain. Breathe this into your heart. Accept it and bless it.

Exhale Blessings

Then imagine breathing out light, joy, and peace to this person. Continue this meditation, breathing in her pain and breathing out light and healing. You may choose to send out the healing by lifting your hands and imagining light radiating from your hands to her.

Loved One

Imagine someone you care deeply about: a loved one, your spouse, your child, or a friend.

Inhale Suffering

Call to mind the ways you know that he is suffering. Breathe this in. Imagine, too, all the ways he is suffering that you are not aware of—perhaps he does not even have words for it.

Exhale Blessings

Breathe out love, light, and good feelings. Continue breathing in his suffering and breathing out love and compassion.

Difficult Relationships

Lastly, call to mind someone who has hurt you or with whom you have a difficult relationship. Imagine for a moment that you drop your armor and your case against her. Just set it aside for now. Imagine seeing this person as her mother might have seen her as a young child. See the hope and potential. Imagine the struggles this person faced as a young person—the same challenges we all face and perhaps even more: being teased, failing at school, being disappointed by a parent or a dream that does not come true. Imagine that suffering and how it may be related to the person you know today.

Inhale Suffering

Now try to imagine the various ways you know this person suffers. If she is prone to anger and harsh words, feel the pain of those actions on the actor. If there is open animosity between you, feel the hurt from the other side. Begin to breathe in this hurt and pain—breathe it into your heart.

Exhale Blessings

Now, breathe out light, gentleness, and hope. Spend some time taking in her pain and sending out goodness and compassion.

LEARNING FIERCE COMPASSION FOR YOURSELF

Perhaps the most difficult person to learn to have compassion for is yourself. Most Westerners seem to have a very confused relationship with themselves. On one hand, we think we are the center of the universe, but if you scratch below the surface, we feel grossly inadequate and even worthless. In another way, these two beliefs make sense; they balance each other out. Perhaps the greatest truth we learn in life is that we can love others only as much as we love ourselves. But where and how to begin?

I have spent most of my life running around trying to make other people happy, so they would like me, and I could finally feel good about myself. I would try to make my parents proud, my teachers impressed, my employers happy, my students satisfied, and my friends and loved ones feel loved. It was a bit like the cat-in-the-hat balancing on a unicycle twirling plates on a stick. The more plates I could juggle, the better I felt about myself. Unfortunately, the cat did a better job than I did. Whenever the plates came crashing down, I felt like a failure. I felt unworthy and unloved. Each fall was a reminder that I had to find a better way. So, I would try to find smaller plates and fewer plates. Eventually, I learned (and am still learning) that there were some plates I did not want to share or get others' opinions on. I did not have to run around trying to make others agree with each other or me. There were parts of my life that were mine, and even if they were imperfect, that was who I was—and it was up to me to accept them.

FIERCE COMPASSION AND HAPPINESS: BECOMING A SPIRITUAL WARRIOR

Fierce compassion is the key that unlocks the door to extraordinary happiness. Quite simply, it teaches you to live life through your heart—not in a sappy, hokey way, but with a fierce courage that comes from knowing that a loving heart can transform all of the darkness and suffering in the world. Knowing that with love, you can transform all things and that there is nothing to fear, to control, or to worry about. You can walk the world in peace and freedom, knowing all will be well because you can make it well. Some call this becoming a *spiritual warrior*, one who no longer fears life because he or she knows the secrets of the heart.

• 8 •

There's No Wrong Way to
Eat a Reese's—Or Is There?

Ethics and Happiness

*A*hh. . . . the Reese's Peanut Butter Cup. My childhood favorite. My Halloween trick-or-treating success was measured by how many of these gold- or orange-foiled treats I received. I counted the mini gold-foiled cups double because somehow the chocolate to peanut butter ratio was more to my liking than in the full-size version. So, when Hershey's launched their ad campaign, "There's no wrong way to eat a Reese's," I was more than happy to research this bold claim. I tried small bites, eat-it-whole bites, chocolate-only bites, peanut butter–only bites, finely sliced bites, pie-shaped bites, hands-free bites, lick-the-wrapper bites, lick-your-finger bites, frozen bites, and slightly melted bites. My scientific investigation concluded that Hershey's was right: There was no wrong way (except if mom discovered you were "experimenting" before dinner). However, I discovered that some ways were better ways than others, and that not all Reese's were created equal. There was something different about those gold-foiled minis that were cut into quadrants. They were better than the rest—and eating them this way definitely cut down my overall consumption. A win-win for everybody, including Mom.

The Reese's slogan raises a more poignant question: Is there a wrong way to do anything? Is there a wrong way—or even a right way—to live? If so, does it make a difference in terms of whether you are happy? Questions of right and wrong, good and bad are the essence of ethical questions. The Buddha included ethical conduct as one of the three areas of the Eightfold Path that leads to the end of suffering; he believed ethical and virtuous conduct was critical for living a life of extraordinary happiness. Apparently, positive psychologists have come to a similar conclusion.

133

POSITIVE PSYCHOLOGY AND THE ETHICAL LIFE

Positive psychologists Christopher Peterson and Marty Seligman approach the question of ethics in two ways. First, they examine which qualities are associated with goodness and the good life across cultures.[1] They refer to these qualities as *virtues* and consider them strengths people can cultivate to increase a sense of meaning and life satisfaction. Second, positive psychologists have studied the *gratifications*, which are similar to pleasures at first glance but are quite different at their core. Both involve a sense of enjoyment. Pleasures bring enjoyment through the senses. On the other hand, gratifications are activities we engage in that bring us a sense of satisfaction, meaning, and purpose—because they are associated with doing something *good*. Thus eating chocolate brings pleasure; buying chocolate for needy children at Christmas time is gratifying. Both may make us feel good, but for very different reasons. Positive psychologists propose that happiness involves pursuing virtuous and gratifying activities rather than just life's pleasures.

POSITIVE PSYCHOLOGY AND VIRTUE

Ethics refers to a system of determining right from wrong in a given community or culture. *Virtues* are the qualities that the community decides are good and should be promoted. Culture can be thought of as the unique set of virtues agreed upon by a group of people: whether a couple, family, community, or country.[2] For example, each cultural group defines how much physical distance between people is "polite" versus "inappropriate," making crowded elevators in international airports an entertaining place to study these cultural differences.

Positive psychologists Seligman and Peterson have studied more than two hundred descriptions of virtues gathered from world religions and the world's greatest thinkers over the past three thousand years. Of course, there were differences, but they also found many commonalities. Although these commonalities took on slightly different forms depending on the time and place, there were six clearly recognizable themes:[3]

- **Wisdom and Knowledge:** Curiosity, perspective, ingenuity, judgment, love of learning, social intelligence

- **Courage:** Valor, perseverance, integrity
- **Love and Humanity:** Kindness, loving
- **Justice:** Citizenship, fairness, leadership
- **Temperance:** Self-control, prudence, humility
- **Spirituality and Transcendence:** Gratitude, hope, forgiveness, humor, zest, appreciation of beauty

The wisest people who have walked the planet have repeatedly said: these are the things that lead to the good, ethical, and happy life. How each is woven into your life's journey and cosmic map is, I believe, an intimate and personal struggle and decision. These are some of the most difficult decisions, those moments that define who we are and where our lives are going. The more mindful we are about each choice, the more likely we are to move toward extraordinary happiness.

TURNING THE TABLES ON VIRTUOUS CONDUCT

Mom and Dad taught us to say "please," "thank you," and "I am sorry." They taught us to clean up after ourselves, to help out when asked, to be polite and respectful to others. When we failed, we were corrected or scolded and were told that our actions were "rude," "impolite," or "inappropriate." In one way or another, we were told that we were hurting *someone else*. But what if I told you that each time you fail to act in a virtuous or ethical way, the person you hurt the most is *yourself?* What if Mom was right about the need to behave in virtuous ways and about the fact that you were hurting others, but never mentioned the most important part? *You are reducing your potential for happiness with each unethical or unkind act.*

I think we misunderstand virtue and ethics because they have been hijacked by parents, teachers, and society to *control* and *manage* the behavior of others rather than promoted as essential for one's personal happiness and well-being—as well as that of everyone else's. When we engage in virtuous activities because we are afraid of being caught or getting in trouble, we are motivated by fear. That does not feed a happy soul. If instead we are motivated to choose virtuous actions because we believe it brings us the happiness we seek—and promotes the happiness of others—then we are motivated for positive reasons. These are two very different types of motivation for the same act.

Although there are many important virtues, many of which have been discussed throughout this book already, I want to focus on three that I think play a particularly important role in the quest for extraordinary happiness: gratitude, humility, and forgiveness.

GRATITUDE AND HAPPINESS

Here's my favorite happiness secret. If you think you may not be cut out for mindfulness, crazy wisdom, or compassion, then gratitude may be the perfect practice for you. Few things can change my state of mind for the good more quickly than making a list of the things for which I am thankful, and there is a good biological reason for this.

Our brain—specifically the limbic system part discussed in chapter 5—is hardwired to focus on danger and all things negative. Why? These things are more likely to kill us. So, bad memories and thoughts naturally stick with us; the good ones easily slip away. Think Velcro for the negative; Teflon for the positive. So you have to put some effort into reminding the brain to track positive events in your life, or it will miscalculate how bad things really are in your life.

In modern society, the problem is that our modern world isn't filled with the physical dangers our brains were designed to protect us against, yet the brain processes psychological threats in the same way it did a saber-toothed tiger. Unfortunately, our brains will naturally focus on all of the negatives *unless we train it not to*. If we can calm our inner lizards and look at the big picture, most of us have far more good than bad in our lives (consider hot water, plentiful food, minimal physical danger, medical care, electricity, cars, air conditioning, the Internet, chocolate, etc.), but the brain will naturally focus more on the bad (such as an unkind comment, work stress, or financial issues) unless we remind ourselves otherwise.

A growing body of research indicates that simple exercises like writing down what you are grateful for each day can have impressive health benefits. More so than compassion, optimism, or hope, gratitude has one of the strongest links to life satisfaction and mental health.[4] Grateful people experience more positive emotions, such as happiness, joy, and enthusiasm. In one U.K. study, researchers found that keeping a daily gratitude journal for two weeks increases participants' sense of well-being, sleep, optimism, and blood pressure.[5] In another, depressed participants who wrote and personally delivered a note of appreciation to someone they had not properly thanked reported improved depressive symptoms for a month.[6] When comparing gratitude journaling to not journaling at all or journaling about one's deepest thoughts and feelings, gratitude journaling significantly improved participants' mental health, whereas expressive journaling and not journaling had no effect.[7] In other words, if you are journaling with the purpose of improving your mood, focus on what you are thankful for, or don't bother.

If I find myself in a low mood, gratitude journaling is one of the first things I use to lift my spirits. For everyday stress, a list with twenty things I am grateful for seems to do the trick. For Thanksgiving, I try to list one hundred things I really appreciate about my partner and kids; the first fifty are easy. After that, I have to dig a bit more, and that really helps to reignite connection and appreciation. It's that push beyond the obvious first few items of thanks that helps the brain recalculate the pros versus cons in your life. So let's try it.

EXERCISE: GRATITUDE JOURNAL

Download worksheet at www.mindfulnessforchocolate.com.

Step 1

List twenty things you are most grateful for in this moment as fast as you can; notice whether your mood seems to lift at a particular point in the process.

1.
2.
3.
4.
5.
6.
7.
8.
9.
10.
11.

12.

13.

14.

15.

16.

17.

18.

19.

20.

Step 2

Take a moment to go down the list and thank someone or something—God, the universe, a person, or your lucky stars—for each one. Stay with each one until you actually feel the warmth of gratitude in your heart.

Step 3

Once you are done, notice how you feel about yourself and life. Do you feel more hopeful? Less stressed? Happier?

Every time I do this exercise, I am surprised at how much more at peace I am with my life. Especially on those days when it seems that everything is going wrong, when I pause to appreciate the handful of things that are going right—or at least have not fallen apart—my whole demeanor changes.

Peterson and Seligman classify gratitude under spirituality and transcendence. So they are not referring to the socially polite habit of saying "please" and "thank you." They are referring to a heartfelt sense of appreciating the kindness of another, the good things we have in life, the beauty that surrounds us. No matter how little you have or how bad things are in life, you can always find something to be grateful for. There is a little mind trick that happens when you begin to notice all the things in your life you are grateful for: suddenly, life is richer. The glass is no longer half empty or half full: it is running over. This is perhaps the easiest step in moving forward to a life of extraordinary happiness.

EXERCISE: CREATING YOUR PERSONAL GRATITUDE HABIT

Download worksheet at www.mindfulnessforchocolate.com.

Becoming a more grateful person is relatively easy if you can find a way to carve out one to five minutes a day to reflect on the things in your life that you appreciate.

Step 1

Identify a current activity that might be a good time to practice gratitude. Common examples include grace before any meal, upon rising, before going to bed, and exchanging gratitude lists with a child or partner before bed.

Option No. 1:

Option No. 2:

Step 2

Implement Option No. 1 for a week. At the appointed time, take a moment to think about or write down everything you are thankful for in that moment. You can use mindfulness to notice the little examples of goodness around you: sunshine through the window, a comfortable chair, or a delicious meal. You can also take a moment to be thankful for the bigger things: the people you love, a job, a comfortable home with air conditioning and central heating—whatever comes to mind that day.

Step 3

If your first option was not a good fit, try your second option or even a third option until being grateful becomes a part of your daily routine.

Step 4

Once you have begun to integrate silent gratitude into your life, try to add telling at least one other person that you appreciate them or something they do each day. Do not be surprised if you find your relationships improve dramatically.

HUMILITY AND THE EGO

The Buddhists say that confusing our true identity with the ego causes our suffering. The ego is the identity we have created—the story we tell ourselves about who we are. For most of us, this is the only identity we know: our profession, family, spouse, children, bank accounts, cars, hobbies, home, religion, culture, and nationalities provide us with this sense of identity. When any of these are threatened, our self is shaken to the core, which is why humans are typically at their worst when their identity is threatened. Divorces bring out the worst in people because it tears at the fabric of multiple aspects of the ego's source of identity. Similarly, threaten a person's mother, religion, or country, and he or she is likely to unleash a whole new side. That is because you are threatening this person's sense of self.

The Buddhist approach to self is quite different. They radically proclaim that, in truth, we have no single core self—that the self the ego protects is nothing more than an illusion. Thich Nhat Hanh explains that the self in best understood as *interbeing*, an identity that is interconnected with everyone and everything else.[8] There is no essential self but rather a sense of self that emerges from the unique combination of these things—fluid, evolving, and a living, interactive part of everything else.

One of my favorite exercises for reflecting on interbeing is considering a loaf of bread and all the people and things that were involved in bringing it to my local store. First, we have grocery store clerks, stockers, and managers, as well as the store itself, the people who built it, and the people who created the materials needed. Then, we have the truck drivers, the truck engineers and builders, the gas stations, roads, and road builders. Of course, farmers, water, earth, seed, and sun were needed to grow the wheat, and numerous machines and their engineers were needed to harvest it. The factory where the bread was made also had to be built, machines engineered, and staff to make it all work. The plastic bag and twist tie required an entirely different set of humans to develop the science, make it practical, and design the art and information to market it. If you want to go further, you can even imagine the first people to develop ovens and bread recipes, and countless thousands who have been a part of breadmaking culture. I think you can see how you can go on and on, until most of humanity and much of the natural world is connected to one loaf: *that* is interbeing. Imagine how much more complex it is with a single person's identity: parents, teachers, friends, enemies, pets, hobbies, career, intergenerational lineage, favorite songs and stories, cultural influences, Instagram feeds, Internet searches, health concerns . . . the list never ends.

When we become attached to the ego's sense of identity, we will suffer because that identity is not real, yet we believe that it is. Many would die defending it if necessary because we confuse the death of the ego as the death of self. So we are devastated when a lover leaves, a parent dies, we lose our job, or something else in our life changes. In those moments, the rug gets pulled out from under the ego and everything comes crashing down. Living from the perspective of the ego is like using a treasure map. Things work fine until difficulties come; then it all falls apart.

If you instead derive your sense of self from interbeing, life unfolds differently. You see yourself as part of the larger whole. You see how you are a part of nature, your family, the company you work for, your friends' lives, the community's life, favorite movies and magazines, your country's happenings, and the evolution of humanity. You can accept the ebb and flow that happen in every life as one is moved in various ways as part of this infinite web of life. As you begin to live your life from a sense of interbeing, you will be humbled—not in the sense that you will finally realize how worthless you are, but more in the sense of deep gratitude for being part of this wondrous and beautiful thing called life.

Perhaps the most important part of being humbled is that it helps you to embrace the good with the not-so-good in yourself and others. You are freed from the prison of seeking approval from others and avoiding their criticism, which is the prison that the ego creates for us. Instead, you are set free, not into the nirvana of perfection, but into the nirvana of being at peace with all that is, all that you are a part of. Even the greatest saints have struggled with this. St. Catherine of Sienna is said to have asked God why there is sorrow and why life isn't easier. The explanation she received was that infinite intelligence allows for all possibilities, including sadness, loss, and darkness.[9] How could the infinite include anything other than everything?

Humility then leads us back to the mystery of the cosmos: Why are things the way they are? Why is there suffering? A humble person says, "I do not know, but I will open my heart to it all—the good and not-so-good that is in me, others, and life." Humility is what happens when you can embrace truth with *gratitude*.

FORGIVENESS

Once you understand humility, forgiveness becomes much easier. As a therapist, I have hundreds of people come to me because they cannot forgive those who have hurt them. Their anger and hurt become their prison. I am asked: How do you forgive a spouse who has cheated on you twice—with the same person? How do you forgive a parent who did not protect you from sexual abuse, even after you told them what was happening? Is it even possible to think about forgiving the father, mother, brother, cousin, uncle, spouse, or stranger who sexually or physically abused you time and time again? What about the friend who betrayed you, the boss who cheated you, or the person who was rude to you at the store?

There are many clichés about forgiveness: "forgive and forget," "forgive but don't forget," and "to err is human; to forgive, divine." All I know is that the only way to truly be liberated from an injustice is to forgive. The only other choice is to live in the prison some refer to as a grudge. A person *holds* a grudge, meaning it takes effort, energy, and intention. To hold a grudge, you have to force your heart to shut off part of the world, part of life. The more grudges you have, the more of life you shut out. When the betrayal was severe, forgiveness may involve avoiding physical contact and may look like a grudge on the outside—but on the inside there is peace and no resentment. This is where humility and compassion come in. When you practice compassion and humility, your heart opens to all of life, to all of life's possibilities.

The benefits of forgiveness for one's mental health have been well established. When people who have been through violence, trauma, or betrayal engage in interventions designed to promote forgiveness, they experience reduced depression, anger, distress, and stress and increased positive mood.[10] Furthermore, those who practice self-forgiveness experience lower levels of anxiety and depression overall.[11] In a dynamic longitudinal study, researchers identified that the measurable decrease in stress that comes with forgiveness accounts for improvement in mental health, thus underscoring the destructiveness of holding a grudge.[12]

No one walks this planet without making mistakes. Unquestionably, some mistakes are more egregious than others. Some people continue to make the same mistake repeatedly, and we need to protect ourselves when they are hurting us or those we love. However, if we choose to hold grudges and fail to forgive, we live in a prison *we* have created and to which only we hold the key.

Perhaps the greatest example of the freedom that forgiveness offers are those who have been physically imprisoned because of their ethnicity and religion and survived the torture of concentration camps, such as the Jews in Nazi Germany or Tibetans in China. Many who were and still are imprisoned and tortured lost hope and became bitter because they were robbed of their former lives or their loved ones were brutally murdered. But there are numerous Jews and Tibetans who have been able to forgive the most heinous acts of which humans are capable. How? They choose to stand against injustice, holding steadfast to the conviction that cruelty comes from ignorance. The wisest who have walked this earth have said, "I too am capable of every evil act." When your heart finally understands this, your heart can never be imprisoned—even if your body is. This type of forgiveness frees you from hatred so that you can be far more effective in challenging and transforming the many injustices in this world.

GRATIFICATIONS AND FLOW

Positive psychologists make a critical distinction between two sources of enjoyment: pleasures and gratifications. *Pleasures* bring us enjoyment through the senses: a great meal, sex, entertainment, or a massage. The *gratifications* bring enjoyment through becoming absorbed and fully engaged in an activity, such as running, painting, reading, or writing. The gratifications are characterized by what is more commonly known as a *flow* experience, a term coined by Hungarian psychologist Mihaly Csikszentmihalyi.

Flow experiences involve being fully absorbed in an activity that suddenly becomes virtually effortless; there is a sense that time is suspended, and you lose sense of yourself, or what the Buddhists might call your sense of ego. You often hear professional athletes describe this sense of flow during a winning touchdown or an Olympic performance. You also hear artists discuss flow when playing music—the music actually plays you—or while painting, dancing, sculpting, acting, or singing. More commonly, many of us experience flow in our daily work experiences when writing a report or doing a particular task: the words and ideas come, but you are not quite sure from where. Flow experiences may not always be "fun" activities, but there is a sense of being moved, sometimes even guided, in your work, activity, or service.

In mystic traditions, flow experiences are understood as those moments when ego gets out of the way and allows divine spirit to move you. You become totally in sync with God, the universe, or however you understand that which is greater than the small self, the ego. All religious traditions have used various forms of meditation, prayer, music, and dance to help practitioners fall in sync with the divine—to achieve a sense of flow.

One thing that characterizes flow experiences—whether a winning pass on the football field, singing in a church choir, or dancing in the middle of the Kalahari—is that the experience always fits neatly within the limits of virtuous behaviors within a given community or culture. Gratifying activities always involve something that is valued and considered beautiful by the person engaging in the activity—it moves you and your life toward the greater good.

Perhaps it is not surprising to learn that people who have more flow experiences are happier and less prone to depression. The ironic part is that people who engage in flow activities actually tend to think that other people are having more fun and are happier. In a classic experiment with teens, Csikszentmihalyi surveyed high-flow and low-flow teenagers.[13] The high-flow teens were active in sports, hobbies, studying, and school activities. The low-flow teens spent their time watching television, playing video games, and hanging out at the mall or movies. Both groups agreed that the low-flow teens were having more fun. But the high-flow kids were the ones who were *actually* happy: They went to college, had meaningful social relationships, and felt a sense of success.

MICROWAVED VERSUS SLOW-COOKED HAPPINESS

Seligman raises a challenging social question regarding gratifications, flow, and depression.[14] He notes that every wealthy nation has experienced a dramatic rise in depression in the past fifty years. The paradox is that virtually every objective indicator of well-being has increased (health, wealth, education, recreation), but our subjective sense of well-being has decreased: We are less happy. He suggests that our wealth has created so many shortcuts to pleasure and momentary happiness that we are not motivated to do the work demanded in the gratifications, which are where we experience flow. You could say that each time we decide to microwave our oatmeal rather than slow cook it like grandmother did, we lose an opportunity to engage in gratifying action. When we habitually choose the microwave over the stovetop in all areas of our lives—work, relationships, health, and finances, as well as cooking—we will experience less gratification, less flow, and less happiness.

MOTORCYCLES, MAINTENANCE, AND JOYRIDING

I wrote this chapter during one of California's extreme heat waves. One Saturday morning, I joined the masses with my laptop in tow to work on this chapter beachside. While sipping my heavily iced tea and writing at an almost beach-front coffee house, a man came up to me and asked, "What are you doing working on a Saturday?" He was dressed in leather from head to toe with the exception of his arms, which were covered with tattoos. Clearly, he was off to enjoy the cool breeze on the Pacific Coast Highway rather than the waves. I smiled and responded, "At least my office *almost* has an ocean view." Then, I wondered to myself: Who was really going to enjoy their day more? I began to ponder if pleasures and gratifications ever mix.

I questioned whether he maintained his bike by himself, perhaps practicing the Zen art of motorcycle maintenance. I imagine it feels different to ride a bike that you take care of by yourself than if you hire someone else to do it. Perhaps the pleasures of the open road are greater if you do the repairs yourself because that pleasure mixes with the gratification of the work you put into it.

In contrast, I sat there typing away in a crowded cafe, watching surfers, bikers, sun worshippers, and fishermen grabbing a cold drink before they hit the beach. As I enjoyed the flow of writing, I periodically took a moment to sit back and mindfully take a sip of my tea, feel the cool ocean breeze on my face, and appreciate the excitement in each person's face—especially the children's—as they prepared for a day of fun. I let myself drink in the beauty of Malibu on a hot summer day. I noticed how much more gratifying gratifications are when you can enjoy the pleasures that come along with them. Ahh . . . perhaps that is the secret.

When pleasure mixes with gratification, there is an exuberant joy. Gratifications without an appreciation of pleasure become hard and joyless work; pleasure without the effort of gratification becomes addiction or leads to meaninglessness and depression. But when you can skillfully balance the two—life is sweeter!

Exercise: Going with the Flow

Download worksheet at www.mindfulnessforchocolate.com.

Most of us have the pleasure principle down but may need more of a nudge with gratifications. Use this exercise to identify where you regularly experience flow and other opportunities to find it.

	Often Experience Flow	Other Opportunities
Sports: Team sports, running, swimming, fishing, hiking, climbing, etc.		
Arts: Dance, music, painting, woodworking, creating anything		
Daily Activities: Cooking, cleaning, shopping, etc.		
Work: Writing, speaking, teaching, calculating, etc.		
Recreation: Reading, volunteering, hobbies, etc.		

List two pleasurable activities you are willing to replace or mix with a gratifying activity.

Pleasure Activity	With Added Gratifying Activity
Example: Watch television after dinner or get takeout for dinner.	Read a good book or cook a meal from scratch once per week.
1.	1.
2.	2.

ONE LAST WORD ON ETHICS

"Anything goes." "It's all good." There is some truth in these familiar expressions. But these do not convey the whole story about what is good. Some choices and actions lead to greater "goods" and happiness than others. Happy people tend to make these choices: when faced with options, they choose to act with virtue and strength to choose gratifying action over simple pleasure. Making virtuous decisions is about trying to choose the best "good"—whatever that may look like in a given situation—when given the option.

Each time you strive toward the good, you take a step closer to happiness. Most of us have rebelled against a large number of classic virtues—such as temperance, perseverance, kindness, citizenship, love of learning, or forgiveness—because these were forced on us as children, often for the sake of others. Ultimately, if you do not—of your own free will—seek to become as virtuous as you can, you cannot find extraordinary happiness. You will have to settle for the ordinary. The paradox is that when you choose virtuous and ethical behavior for its own sake—for your own sake—you finally find freedom.

CHOCOLATE MEDITATION NO. 3: THERE'S NO WRONG WAY TO EAT A REESE'S—OR IS THERE?

OK. Let's have some fun. Let's try to combine the pleasure of eating chocolate with the gratification of wisdom: curiosity and love of learning. Find a peanut butter cup or similar type of chocolate or treat. And then go ahead and conduct the childhood experiment I conducted. The hypothesis under investigation is that there is no wrong way to eat a Reese's. Let's call this the *null* hypothesis: there is no difference between the various options for eating a peanut butter cup. The *alternative* hypothesis is that there is a difference. Experiment with any of these and other options:

- Eating different parts: chocolate only, peanut butter only, eating it whole, in different-shaped pieces
- Eating it at different temperatures: room temperature, chilled, frozen, warm, melted
- Eating off of different things: fingers, the wrapper, a plate
- Eating it in different places: in the pool, on a swing, on a horse
- Eating it at different times: before breakfast, after lunch, before bedtime
- Eating while doing different things: watching a movie, sitting at the beach, with the one you love

Let your childlike imagination come up with all the different ways to eat a peanut butter cup. Laugh. Play. Think outside the box. If you play with this scientific investigation seriously, you may learn more about the art of mixing gratifying activity with simple pleasure—using a touch of crazy wisdom.

· 9 ·

Artificial Chocolate and Comfort Foods

Dangers and Pitfalls on the Path

𝒯he path to extraordinary happiness may be paved in chocolate, but I never said it was easy or without danger. Let's face it: If it were simple and easy, you would not need to read this book. You—and most everyone—would be able to find your way with little guidance or effort. Getting off track is common. Some settle for the "small" or what comes easily, whether a second-rate career, relationship, or other life goal. Others decide that the comforts of ordinary happiness are better than facing the changes that come with pursuing extraordinary happiness. Some are afraid of how others will react. Still others fall prey to ego tricks and continue to take life too seriously: for them, even fun is hard work. Even with the best of intentions and plans, you may find yourself entangled with a snake. These pitfalls are common and perhaps necessary on the path of true joy: a state where happiness emanates from within rather than being triggered by outside circumstances.

ARTIFICIAL CHOCOLATE: SETTLING FOR WHAT IS EASY

If you are setting the height of a basketball hoop so that a child develops self-esteem, where would you set it? Should the child make a basket 100 percent of the time? Eighty percent? Fifty percent? The answer surprised me: 50 percent. At 50 percent, you gain a sense of competency and confidence in your abilities that you do not develop when it is easier or harder to reach your goal. Nonetheless, we live in a time when most parents expect their child to win every time.[1] If you do doubt this, check out any of your local children's sporting leagues and watch the behaviors of parents when their child's team loses. When winning comes easily and is guaranteed, we actually have *less* confidence in our abilities because we did not earn our success. We know we are fakes, and so doubt creeps in. Even worse, we learn to view our abilities as inherent or "fixed" characteristics (referred to as fixed mind-set) rather than competences that were developed through effort and practice (growth mind-set), creating a sense of helplessness to pursue our dreams.[2]

Many of us learned early that losing was bad or even unacceptable. For some, this means that it is safer to not try at all rather than risk the humiliation of losing. After all, if you try and fail, you *prove* you are a loser. If you do not try, it is always theoretically possible that you are not a loser. Others of us prefer to only play when we are guaranteed to win 95 percent of the time. That is relatively safe for our egos. But we always know in the back of our minds that there is a bigger court we could be playing on—one where we may not win every game, but where we will learn more and grow. This is how we end up settling for artificial chocolate—for ordinary happiness. It is not bad, but deep inside we know there is something better out there. As you embark on this journey toward extraordinary happiness, you need to ask yourself: Where have I settled for ordinary happiness? My career? My relationship? My health?

In my practice as a therapist, most people come to see me because they have "settled" in some way. Some have settled for comfortable yet passionless marriages: ten years and three kids later, they are depressed. Some have settled for pseudo-peace rather than rocking the boat with their spouse or families, and now they feel imprisoned in their relationships. Some have settled for either a safe or lucrative career, but now feel that their lives have no meaning or purpose. Some have settled for fun and partied their way through their teens, twenties, and even thirties, and now are wondering where their life is going and why they let their dreams slip through their fingers. Settling is one of the easiest ways to get off course.

EXERCISE: RAISING THE BAR ON HAPPINESS

Download worksheet at www.mindfulnessforchocolate.com.

In what areas of your life do you tend to settle and play it safe?

_____ Relationships/friendships

_____ Career/work/school

_____ Health/sports

_____ Adventures/fun/travel

_____ Other hopes and dreams

Take it up a notch: *Describe one small step you could take to get closer to where you want to be (e.g., take a small risk, try something new, address a problem you are avoiding):* _____

COMFORT FOODS AND ORDINARY HAPPINESS

Chocolate sounds great—extraordinary happiness and enlightenment even better. So why not just dig in? What are you waiting for? Well, there is wisdom in hesitation. Our social circles have a set point for happiness, and those who attempt to proceed beyond the permissible amount of happiness often receive little support or encouragement from family, friends, or employers. I would be lying to say that the road to extraordinary happiness is easy, even if chocolate sustains you throughout the journey. Those who dare to venture beyond the social norms for happiness soon learn that extraordinary happiness is a rebellious act in our society. It is wise to proceed with a certain amount of caution.

Each social group includes a set of norms for how much happiness is permissible by its members and how it should be expressed. For example, many friendships are built on a common enemy or something to complain about. When you lose this common enemy or stop complaining about the same problem, the relationship often falters. Many single women's relationships involve looking for "Mr. Right" together; when one of those women actually finds him, there is often tension in the relationship with friends who still are looking. The "lucky" woman's happiness is often not greeted with sympathetic joy but jealousy or worse. The loss of a common problem creates a separation that is often irreparable.

I recently had two different friends who had the opportunity to quit their jobs to spend more time with their children. What type of response did they get from their family and friends? Would you believe it was an overwhelming amount of disapproval, guilt, and disdain? My friends arrived at a point in their lives where they could live their dreams—the dreams many of us share—and many of their employed friends withdrew support.

Research on lottery winners reveals a similar problem.[3] Within a year, most are back to their same level of happiness or lower. The greatest stressor: the change in their social relationships. The change in financial status suddenly changes the power dynamic in all of their personal, family, social, and work relationships—no one sees them the same way anymore, and they often expect a lot more than ever before—not to mention the stress of managing large amounts of money, taxes, and the media. The effect is so dramatic that risk of suicide for lottery winners actually increases.

INVITATION TO DISCOMFORT

As you break the barriers of ordinary happiness, you are outside the norm—at the outer edge of the bell curve. This will make some people feel uncomfortable. In these moments, you have a choice: do you retreat to make others and yourself comfortable, or do you risk the discomfort? But discomfort is required to learn new ways to experience joy, which is one of the reasons meaningful education is always uncomfortable. My career as a professor has taught me that.

I am one of those professors whom you either love or avoid at all costs. Students rarely have a neutral reaction to me. Why? Because I do not retreat to the ordinary and instead invite students to move beyond their comfort zones into the new and the extraordinary. It would be easier for me and them to settle for the ordinary, to stay within the comfort of the bell curve. It would take less time to prepare my lectures and class exercises. I would spend less time in office hours encouraging students when the voices of self-doubt and fear haunt them. I would spend fewer weekends grading complex and challenging papers. My students would spend more of their weekends having fun and less time reading, writing, and pushing themselves beyond the limits they have set for themselves.

Usually, around week twelve of the sixteen-week semester, we hit a crisis point, when students get scared. It is the worst part of my job— hearing their frustration and pleas to make things easier. I know my job at this point is to help them relax into their discomfort of the semester's challenge and trust that they will rise. Why? Because I know they will, and then I will get the calls. I always do. Within a couple of years, I hear how that "scary" assignment in my class set them up to get licensed, a paid presentation gig, or a major promotion. These calls come frequently from the students who were the most scared. That is when my gift becomes clear. My gift is a taste of the extraordinary life.

Similar to the task parents face in raising functional adults, I find it helpful to view each student in my class and each person who comes to me in therapy as having two parts. One is asking for comfort, to reassure them that they are OK just the way they are. The other part knows they need to grow to create a better life. The easy route is to attend only to one part or the other, offering either comfort or challenge. The hard road is to do both simultaneously—knowing when to push and when to support so that they feel strong enough to take the risks that are necessary in seeking an extraordinary life.

One of the things that helps them most is that I avoid giving my approval as much as possible. Instead, I push, nudge, and encourage my students and clients to be the judge of their lives and their worthiness. When they no longer look to someone else for approval but themselves, then they are finally free—free from the tyranny of the ordinary. Ordinary is just another name for what everyone else is doing, for what is common. When you learn to hear your inner voice as clearly as you hear the outer voices (it is important to pay attention to both), that is when you start moving toward the extraordinary.

SPIRITUAL MATERIALISM AND
TAKING HAPPINESS TOO SERIOUSLY

I have met dozens of them. Dozens of American Buddhists who are far more accomplished meditators than I. They have been to Asia and studied for months or even years. They go on long silent meditation retreats and spend hours with their teachers. They can quote ancient Buddhist texts with remarkable insight and memory. But then I look into their eyes, and I do not see it. The smile. The light. The joy that is the intended fruit of such labor. If you are not laughing, you still have not found the path, even if it looks like you are on it.

There is a danger on the spiritual path that Buddhist teacher Chogyam Trungpa calls *spiritual materialism*.[4] Spiritual materialism can happen in any religious tradition. I am sure you have seen it. Someone at your church, temple, or meditation circle who is serious, dedicated, and enthusiastic yet is also someone with whom you would be hesitant to share a bad day or problem. Why? Because you are likely to get some sugar-coated advice that says if you just pray, meditate, or think positively, it will all go away. That is what they believe and how they live their lives.

Spiritual materialism involves pretending or dissociating from the bad and pretending to be good and see only good. It's an attempt at a shortcut to the extraordinary—but there isn't any. Spiritual materialism is easy to see in someone else but more difficult to see in yourself—because when it is you, you can see the effort you are putting into life (which is more a form of repressing and denying what is), and so it feels as if you are on the right path. It certainly feels as if you are on a more productive path than when you live inside the bell curve and are settling for ordinary happiness. In fact, you take extraordinary happiness very seriously—actually you take it *too* seriously. The danger is that this path looks and feels extraordinary, but it is just another form of artificial chocolate.

How do you know whether you are taking happiness too seriously? This is a tough question because it is hard to know at times. I think the answer goes back to: do you laugh at yourself often and heartily? If you are laughing, if your heart can feel lightness even in the darkest of moments, you are on the path to extraordinary happiness. If not, you may need to adjust your course. This is where crazy wisdom keeps you from becoming truly crazy.

AVOIDING SNAKES AND THINGS THAT BITE

A surprising danger on the path are the snakes who seek out the warmth of those who have the glow of extraordinary happiness. Like reptilian serpents who hunt using infrared to identify body heat, these human snakes have an uncanny ability to sense your joy and how it differs from that of others. Although these folks are initially some of the most charming, generous, and "loving" people you will ever meet, their masks eventually slip, revealing their cold-blooded nature. By the time that happens, you are hopelessly trapped in their coils, wondering how you ended up in such a wild predicament. Mental health professionals diagnose such humans as having "disordered" or "abusive" personalities, such as narcissism or antisocial personality (sociopaths). Those who have many of their traits but do not qualify for the full diagnosis cause less damage, but their bite still stings. In her book *Dodging Energy Vampires*,

Dr. Christiane Northrup refers to both the severe and more mild versions of these characters as "energy vampires," because they will suck the life out of you, much in the same way as mosquitos and pythons.[5]

Early in my career as a therapist, I didn't believe such humans existed, even though they were documented in research and diagnostic manuals. I naively believed a well-trained "compassionate" therapist like myself could save anyone. I didn't believe anyone consciously chose cruelty, at least not consistently, or actually lacked a conscience. Thankfully, my sincere desire to understand humanity and my willingness to be humbled enabled me to see a reality I was afraid to believe could be true. Reality is a great teacher if you are willing to learn the lessons, which were painful, both personally and in the lives of my clients. Although I have not given up on the idea that such persons have a divine purpose and are not truly evil, from a simply practical perspective, it is wise to learn how to quickly identify these folks and skillfully disentangle yourself. I've seen many lives ravaged by ignorance about such characters. Please note that a formal mental health diagnosis requires a licensed health professional to actually observe and interact with the person being diagnosed. Thus, neither you nor I can do so with this chapter alone.

The personality types that are most likely to be drawn to you on the path to extraordinary happiness are the following:

- **Borderline Personality Disorder:** Most frequently female, these folks have notable instability in mood, identity, relationships, and behavior, tending to see things in black and white or people as all good or all bad. In addition to unparalleled charm, they manipulate with guilt, blame, and even harming themselves to reestablish reconnection because they need the other to maintain a sense of self. Most people diagnosed with this condition were severely abused as children and—if they are open to change—can often be treated successfully using evidence-based approaches, such as dialectical behavior therapy.[6] However, it is important to note that the vast majority of people who have been abused do not develop this disorder. People who qualify for the diagnosis are often also diagnosed with other conditions, such as depression (96 percent), anxiety disorder (88 percent), and substance use disorders (50 percent).

- **Narcissistic Personality Disorder:** Receiving considerable recent attention with the rise of social media, narcissists require unceasing admiration from others yet lack sincere empathy. They are predominantly male, often taking the form of the fairytale "Prince Charming" or the more obvious "Casanova." Although they can be quite charming, they quickly become manipulative and demanding in relationships, believing that they are entitled to special treatment. Unfortunately, that special treatment does not include psychotherapy; thus they rarely seek or respond well to mental health interventions. Narcissists frequently suffer from depression—when the world does not reflect their sense of worth—and substance use disorders.

- **Antisocial Personality Disorder (or "Sociopath" in Criminal Justice Literature):** Antisocial personality involves many of the same traits as narcissistic personality disorder but is more severe due to affected individuals' lack of a conscience. In *The Sociopath Next Door,* Harvard psychologist Dr. Martha Stout explains that most sociopaths are not violent, but rather are master manipulators who prey on the compassion of kindhearted people with the "pity play."[7] By definition incapable of empathy and fundamentally lacking a conscience, sociopaths use whatever words, emotions, or behaviors serve their purpose at that moment. They are frequently male and often have a history of violence. The more intelligent they are, the more sophisticated their strategies and methods and the more difficult to identify early when meeting them. Most experts see little hope for successful treatment if the person has the full disorder. More than 90 percent of people qualifying for the full disorder have other mental health issues, such as substance misuse, depression, and anxiety.

Although there are several other possible personality disorders, these three are the most likely to gravitate toward those living lives of extraordinary happiness because—and this is still hard for me to believe—they want to siphon off your joyousness, generous spirit, and kindheartedness. More crudely put, they are "takers" looking for someone who has much to give. These disorders are difficult even for the experts to accurately diagnose, so we have few reliable statistics. The most respected researchers estimate that 3 to 15 percent of the population qualifies for one of these three disorders, with 9 percent cited as a reasonable middle ground. When considering those who have many features but not a full-blown disorder, Dr. Northrup estimates that 20 percent of the population have many of these characteristics—which translates to one in five people. Even at the most conservative estimate of 3 percent, that is ten million Americans who could cause you significant trouble on your journey; at 9 percent, that means we have nearly thirty million snakes to manage. Additionally, people in the active phases of addiction often have many of these characteristics as well. So, keep your eyes peeled and watch your step—there are a lot of snakes out there. You have surely tangled with several already.

HOW TO SPOT A SNAKE

Unfortunately, it is not easy to identify these personality disorders early in a relationship, whether romantic, friendship, or professional. Typically, the symptomatic behaviors are not visible until (a) you have an established long-term relationship with the individual, and (b) you disappoint or anger the person in some way. Until then, you may have no idea that you are dealing with a snake. Of course, you will also meet people who have some of these *characteristics*, making them difficult people, but ultimately they are more workable. For example, many people going through a divorce will exhibit some or all of these behaviors, but it is not a pervasive pattern in multiple relationships in their lives. To formally qualify for the mental health disorder, these patterns need to be *pervasive, inflexible patterns* across a broad range of personal and social relationships and cause significant distress and impairment in important areas of functioning. Thus your ex may have demonstrated some of these "features" but may not qualify for the actual disorder unless there is a string of others who have received the same treatment. The injured are usually not hard to find.

EARLIEST POSSIBLE WARNING SIGNS

These folks are not hard to identify once you know what to look for. The difficult part is to spot them initially. The more skilled you become at early detection, the fewer entanglements you will have. My clients and I have collected a list of the earliest warning signs—yellow flags—that were easily excused in the first few months of dating, of friendship, or at work:

- **Absolute Charm:** Initially, snakes are the most charming, helpful, amazing, giving, loving people you have ever met (note: this will change). In romantic relationships, they may "love bomb," showering you with chocolates and flowers, planning romantic evenings, and communicating incessantly. They are the most romantic, into-you people you have ever dated. It's hard to believe they are real—because they are not. Even if it is not fully conscious on their part, this charm is a clever ploy to draw you into their tangled web.
- **"Too" Perfect:** In romantic relationships, they sweep you off your feet and move the relationship along fast. They are "perfect" partners, often because they read your profile online, learned what you wanted, and are freakily morphing into exactly what you "dreamed of." They try to form a fast bond of trust and excitement, which they will soon use to manipulate and control you. If you complain about a habit or situation, they fix it immediately. Sometimes, after the wedding, this façade immediately fades once it is no longer necessary to keep you in the relationship. I know several people for whom this happened as soon as the honeymoon—chilling.
- **Over-Giving:** Similarly, whether a romantic partner, platonic friend, or new colleague, they may dazzle you with their helpfulness and generosity in the beginning, creating a sense of indebtedness that is hard for you to later deny. They sense that you are someone who will give once generously given to.
- **Splitting:** They tend to see people and events as all good or all bad. You are either friend or foe, and memories are all positive or all negative. Their ability to empathize with multiple perspectives is severely impaired, which is often noticeable in early conversations if you listen carefully.
- **Victim Mentality:** Perhaps one of the easiest early warning signs to detect, people with these personalities always see the outside world as the source of their problems. The first few accounts of victimization typically sound realistic, and—because

you are kindhearted—you have sympathy for their plight. But you may notice that they take virtually no responsibility for their part of creating the mess or getting out of it. If they do, it is mostly intellectually describing their teeny-tiny contribution to the situation or talking about how they would fix things if only . . . oops, another roadblock and something or someone else to blame. Once you know what to listen for, the pattern becomes clear long before the mask slips.

- **Drama:** Especially characteristic of the borderline, you will notice that their life is constantly in crisis. Even a simple slight from a friend can turn into a drawn-out, woe-is-me pity-fest for days. As soon as one drama is resolved, something else happens to start a new battle in a new arena. Some need to always be fighting with at least one person, which provides a sense of identity and purpose. Even though they convincingly deny enjoying any of it, they constantly create it. When they are without drama, they feel lost and adrift. So the next battle begins. And soon, it will be with you.
- **Words versus Actions:** Another early sign is that their words and actions don't always match. They describe themselves as "easygoing," but you notice from how they treat the waitstaff or handle a delay that they really aren't. They profess their love repeatedly and love bomb, but they don't actually seem to have heartfelt empathy for you and your needs, such as time with your best friend or a night alone. When you confront them, they have a solid, logical excuse to explain away the inconsistency—but it is never a good sign.

CLEAR SIGNS THAT YOU ARE DEALING WITH A SNAKE

The longer you are in a relationship with this type of person, the more characteristic patterns start to surface, and you finally know what you are dealing with:

- **Entitlement:** A clear sense of entitlement emerges, believing their needs and desires are more important than yours, even if they *verbally* say otherwise. They will regularly put down individuals or whole classes of people. Their endless needs and demands become overwhelming.

- **Punishment:** If you fail to provide them with the attention, privileges, or rights to which they believe they are entitled, they will harshly or in a passive-aggressive way punish you by withholding affection, blaming, ignoring, or whatever they think will hurt you the most. If the first tactic does not work, they will try another until you capitulate.
- **Lack of Empathy and Callousness:** Especially prevalent in narcissism and sociopathy, these people display no true empathy, having little awareness or care about how their behavior affects others. They may verbally say they care, but then they use this knowledge of your emotions to further manipulate rather than support you.
- **Control:** Although they may deny it with their words, their actions reveal that they must be in control or they become hostile, pouty, or rude. It's their way or no way. If they cannot get you to behave by being nice, they get mean.
- **Poor Boundaries:** All personality disorders have poor boundaries. Borderlines expect you to feel and take on their pain and make it better. Narcissists and sociopaths believe they are entitled to take what you have. Essentially, your agency, thoughts, and needs matter little.
- **Deflecting Criticism and Crazy-Making:** One of the clearest, brightest, neon signs that you found a snake: if you dare to point out their bad behavior or how you got hurt, they will deflect the criticism and turn the conversation into an attack on you, often resorting to "you're too sensitive" or "crazy." Before you know it, *you* are the only one apologizing. You often end interactions wondering "What just happened?" and questioning your sanity. This is the crux of the abuse. Once they get you to doubt yourself, it becomes nearly impossible to pull yourself out of the twisted web without professional—or an amazing friend's—help.
- **Mood Swings and Eggshells:** Individuals with any of these personality types are prone to severe mood swings and anger when others do not conform to their expectations and demands. If you are naturally an empathetic person, you will soon

find yourself walking on eggshells to avoid triggering an argument or similar "event."

- **Personality Shifts—Dr. Jekyll and Mr. Hyde:** They may have swift shifts of personality, from gregarious and lighthearted to rageful in a second, often reserving their worst behavior for those closest to them. Their charm can be so convincing that the outside world can't believe what happens behind closed doors.
- **Pathological Lying:** Characteristic of many sociopaths and narcissists, they sincerely believe the lies they tell. These are the people who can fool a lie detector test—and the rest of us. Some lie for sport, but most lie to get you to believe a particular image of them. Once you find one such lie (e.g., cheating, events that didn't happen as they said), you'll often find more.
- **Other Psychopathology:** Depression and anxiety are common when the world fails to reflect their inflated or preferred sense of self. Substance abuse is frequent as a way to cope with their chaotic (borderline) or empty (narcissist/sociopath) inner worlds. Borderlines frequently self-harm and threaten suicide.

HOW TO SAVE YOURSELF

My entire career is premised on the belief that people can change. The vast majority can. After many years of hoping for better outcomes, I must concede that this 9 percent of humanity doesn't change that much or very often. Actually, there is hope for the borderline personality with the right treatment and if the person wants to change. But if you are dealing with someone who may be a full-blown narcissistic or antisocial personality, you should consider a new approach to setting boundaries, and possibly running. I spent many years hoping to offer different advice, but the research and my twenty-five years of clinical and personal experience make it clear that you may be in danger. So let's consider your options:

- **Romantic Partner, No Children:** If you are dating, engaged, or married without children and you believe your partner has a severe abusive personality that he or she won't get treated, find yourself a good therapist and figure out whether salvaging the relationship is realistic. If you decide to go, you may need to strategize how to leave without being physically hurt if your partner has a severe form of these disorders.

- **Romantic Partner, with Children:** If there is no violence or other severe behavior, you may want to consider seeking couples' therapy with a highly skilled therapist (you might explore one of the only evidence-based couples' therapies, emotionally focused couples' therapy, at www.icceft.com) and proceed with caution. In some cases, you too will need to leave for the sake of the children. The research is clear: children do better when they are not living in a home with severe personality disorders, conflict, or violence. If the symptoms are mild or more situational, you may be able to turn things around.
- **Family Member:** Many of us have parents, siblings, or other family members who fit the description of a snake. In this case, find yourself a good therapist who can help you set healthy boundaries (don't settle for a therapist who simply joins in bad-mouthing your family with you). Complete cutoff is rarely the answer, but crystal-clear boundaries really make a difference. I have worked with many clients who have been able to significantly improve their relationship with a parent or sibling diagnosed with a personality disorder.
- **Friend:** If you find that your friend drains your energy constantly or manipulates you, it is OK to leave—even after "all" they have done for you. If they have an actual personality disorder, they did it to put you in this exact "guilted and paralyzed" position.
- **Coworker:** Try to distance yourself politely and keep clear boundaries. Most human resource rules will protect you.
- **Boss:** Having a boss with such traits puts you in a tricky situation. Depending on how hard it is to find a similar position and the protections at your workplace, you may find seeking a new position is worth it. Or, you may find changing your expectations and learning how to handle such a personality is enough to make your position still work for you.
- **Self:** If one of the signs above reminded you of something you do, it's worth talking with a professional, such as a dialectical behavior therapist, to see if you can make changes.

Bottom line: it's difficult to find sustained happiness if you are living in a viper's nest.

HAPPINESS AND JOYFUL DISCIPLINE

The potential dangers on the path can be summed up by realizing that extraordinary happiness is a discipline—a joyful one. It is like learning to ride a bike without training wheels. You get your balance and ride for a few feet and then fall. Get up again, ride some more, until you fall again. Each time you go for a longer and longer time. But it takes discipline each time you fall. You must tell yourself to get up and try again. In one moment, it is easy and you are flying; the next moment you cannot figure out how you hit the ground. When you feel the ebb and flow: that *is* it! Do not be afraid each time you hit the ground. It is not a sign that you are doing it all wrong. It is a sign that you are on the path. Most people think that when they are on the right path it should be easy and effortless. No, that is farthest from the truth. Lives of extraordinary happiness are *anything but* effortless—otherwise, such lives would be ordinary. So if you find yourself falling, it is a good sign that you might be on the right track. The trick is to pick yourself up and try again.

• *10* •

The Art of Savoring

Joyfulness as a Way of Life

I could not finish it: the Sacher torte, perhaps the most famous chocolate cake in the world. I was savoring it at its point of origin: the Sacher
Hotel. I rarely fail to take full advantage of any fine chocolate presented
to me. But this day was different. It was Sunday morning in Salzburg,
Austria, home to not only Mozart and *The Sound of Music* but also more
than fifty churches, enduring reminders of the years it served as a seat
for archbishops. But that morning the sound of the city's least celebrated
music filled my soul. There was no room left for cake.

On Sunday mornings, the bells ring. They ring from grand cathe-
drals and tiny chapels: some deep and mellow, others high and tinny;
some slow and deliberate; others with a spring in their swing. On the
Sabbath, they do not ring on the hour but each in its own time, mark-
ing the end or beginning of a service or special occasion. Nonetheless,
at times, they seem to be answering each other in impromptu harmony.
One sings out, and within a minute another joins and then another and
another until the hills are alive with music and all earthly sounds are
hushed by the choir of bells. One by one, their voices fade until one
lone soul signals its final *Auf wiedersehen*. Then the sounds of everyday
life trickle back.

In earlier times, the bells set the rhythm for life in this literal cow
town. When they rang, farmers knew when it was time to awaken, eat
lunch, return home, celebrate, and mourn. Centuries later, on Sundays
the bells are still a call to remember God and all that is holy. As I sat on
the Sacher Hotel terrace, sipping tea specially blended for this distinctive
cake, I heard the bells ring and clearly received their call to remember

that which is greater than myself. When their voices faded, I listened as the sounds of daily life returned: traffic droning, dogs barking, trains rumbling, and friends chattering—all humming along as they always do, as if nothing sacred had just happened.

I sat watching the holy and mundane dance, each needing the other for their voice to be heard. Life was whole. One could not exist without the other. That morning, I saw that each was beautiful and sacred in its own way. Surely, the roaring buses and cars would be seen as miraculous to the city's first inhabitants, Celts from 7,000 BC. Similarly, the chorus of church bells inspired awe in this twenty-first-century California girl. The miraculous, the ordinary, the sacred, the profane: they are just a matter of perception determined by what is familiar. The secret is being able to see the dance between ordinary and extraordinary, which is the dance of life.

CHOCOLATE AND WALNUTS

A Rumi poem tells the story of a man who climbs high in a walnut tree and drops walnuts into the pool below. A reasonable man walks by saying, "You'll regret this. The nuts will be gone by the time you get down." The man in the tree replies, "I'm not here for walnuts: I want the music they make when they hit."[1] By now, you have discovered my secret truth: chocolate is my walnut. Just like the man in Rumi's poem, it is not the taste I seek but the soulful inspiration chocolate offers. Chocolate has become for me—and hopefully at this point for you—a reminder of how to live life well: mindfully, with purpose and an open heart. If you have read this far and played with some of the exercises, by now there is no way to eat chocolate as you did in the past. Chocolate is now a call, a reminder to live differently. Thankfully, chocolate is virtually everywhere, so your world is now filled with quiet reminders of how to seek a life of extraordinary happiness.

As you begin to cultivate the art of extraordinary happiness, you begin to discover *joy*. Joy to me is a feeling that comes from within, whereas happiness, in its ordinary sense, is usually triggered by something in the outside world. When happiness becomes a learned skill, joy is the result. When it comes over you, it is unmistakable.

EATING LIFE WHOLE: EMBRACING JOY AND SORROW

If there is a single secret that those who live extraordinary happiness share, it is this: you must eat life whole. The good and the bad, the joys and the sorrows, the ups and downs, chocolate and lima beans. They go together, and there is no escaping the painful moments. Those you love will die; you will experience failure; tragedy will strike; your heart will break. But all will be OK—because joy will inevitably return, just as sure as pain, just as certain as the sun and moon do their dance each day and the bells in Salzburg ring. When that finally melts into your soul—when deep in your being you understand this—your life changes and will never be the same. This may be life's greatest paradox: when you finally embrace the suffering in your life, you no longer suffer—at least not in the same way, and certainly less and less the more your heart understands this basic truth.

HOW TO EAT CHOCOLATE LIKE A BUDDHA: MAKING JOY A WAY OF LIFE

How do you make joy a way of life? At first, most of us envision monumental changes that seem impossible to achieve. In truth, the journey is not as hard or obscure as it initially seems. By making small changes— five minutes here and there—your daily reality soon shifts. The Buddhists also encourage creating a *sangha*, a group of friends who share the spiritual journey. When we unite, our journeys are easier and burdens lighter than when we travel alone. Finally, we find ways to keep the joys of life—such as eating chocolate—alive and central to each day.

SMALL STEPS TO BIG CHANGES

At this point, I hope you have found one or two things in this book that resonate with you, things you think you might want to try integrating into your everyday life. The one thing I do not want you to do is to try to start doing them all at the same time. Pick one thing and start with that. Once that becomes habit, try adding another. Changing everything all at once is *not* a recipe for success. In his book *Do One Thing Different,* solution-oriented therapist Bill O'Hanlon explains how making one, easy, doable small change typically begins a cascade of positive changes by interrupting the old mindless patterns, allowing you to make fresh, new choices.[2] Radically forcing change by reengineering your entire life all at once rarely results in lasting change.

The paradox is that small changes often make a huge impact, much like a single pebble thrown into a lake. The reverberations stretch out far beyond the impact point of the pebble. That is exactly what happens when you start to make changes in your life. Each little change finds its way to touch multiple aspects of your life. So, go ahead and see if a chocolate a day makes a difference in your life.

EXERCISE: A CHOCOLATE A DAY IS ALL IT TAKES

Download worksheet at www.mindfulnessforchocolate.com.

If you have not done so already, it is time to pick one pebble from this book and try to put it into action in your everyday life.

Step 1

Buy a box of your favorite chocolate (or similar treat), enough for seven days.

Step 2

Choose one exercise, meditation, or activity from this book that you would like to put into practice. Begin by putting a ✓ next to items you might want to try and an × next to things that do not appeal to you right now. Then, rank order your three favorites by putting 1, 2, and 3 next to them.

- ☐ Chocolate meditation no. 1: mindfulness eating meditation using chocolate
- ☐ Mindfulness meditation with a breath focus (1 to 5 minutes)
- ☐ Dishwashing, walking, or daily activity meditation
- ☐ Crazy wisdom: placing a piece of chocolate somewhere surprising each day
- ☐ Crazy wisdom: a dose of daily play
- ☐ Crazy wisdom: a koan a day keeps (in)sanity at bay
- ☐ Compassion meditation no. 1: loving-kindness
- ☐ Compassion meditation no. 2: a day in the life
- ☐ Compassion meditation no. 3: stranger, friend, enemy
- ☐ I-Thou encounter with a stranger
- ☐ Gratitude: find one to five minutes per day to be grateful for the good things in your life.
- ☐ An original idea that came to you: _____

Step 3

Tell someone that you are committing yourself to doing this activity and see if they will join you in your new activity and/or put a reminder in your favorite digital device.

Step 4

Put the chocolate or reward somewhere you can see it. It will be your reminder to do your task. *You may have a chocolate only if you complete your task.* Consider it bribery or inspiration; I do not care which. Just keep your promise to have a chocolate only if you complete your task. Obviously, if chocolate does not motivate you, you should find a good substitute that will work for you. If you have a child or partner, you may want to get two chocolates per day; they can have theirs only if you do your exercise. Sometimes it helps to have those you love "invested" in your success.

Step 5

Do it.

Step 6

Once this task seems well integrated into your life, perhaps two to three weeks, add the next one. Act. Snack. Repeat. Continue until you are the one telling your friends about the difference between ordinary and extraordinary happiness.

CREATING YOUR OWN PERSONAL SANGHA

You may find extraordinary happiness by yourself, but it is always an easier journey when shared. As we have discussed, extraordinary happiness is a rebellious act—you are moving beyond the set parameters for happiness in our culture. Building a network of chocolate connoisseurs is the surest way to keep yourself on track.

Buddhists refer to a group of people who come together to support each other on the spiritual journey as a sangha. Traditionally, a sangha is headed by a monk or other religious figure. If you do not already belong to a sangha, congregation, or spiritual group of some sort, you can create your own sangha with people who are already in your life.

Friends and Family

So where do you start? Friends and family are usually the first choice. Are you already close to someone you believe has a greater understanding of extraordinary happiness than yourself? That would be the best person to start with. If not, who among your family and friends might be interested in joining you on your journey? How might you entice them? Does chocolate give you any ideas?

Children

Do you have children or spend much time with children? They are often like little Buddhas, living more fully in the moment than most adults. Many practice gratitude more readily than adults, enjoying a butterfly's visit, the flower their parent might consider a weed, or the rainbows made from the sprinklers. Spend some time each week blowing bubbles, making up songs, or playing imaginary games with a child. They may help you remember some of the wisdom you lost long ago.

Spiritual and Religious Groups

Do you already belong to a spiritual or religious group? Did you at one time? All spiritual and religious traditions have wisdom and guidance to offer on the path to extraordinary wisdom *plus* most offer a built-in sangha. You may need to join a study group or volunteer if you belong to a large church or temple to get the type of support you need. You may even want to start a small discussion or dinner group with people from your place of worship.

Dead and Living Poets

One of the richest additions to my sangha is to read and listen to the words of others who are students of extraordinary happiness. For me, the poetry and writings of Rumi, St. Francis, the Dalai Lama, St. John of the Cross, and Martin Luther King Jr.—as well as playlists that remind me of the good in humanity and life—provide inspiration. Through their various arts, they share their struggles, and I learn how to better handle mine. Their words also provide encouragement when it would be easier to settle for ordinary happiness and the comfort of the bell curve and mindless pleasure.

Virtual Sanghas

If you look around your life and cannot find the support you need, you may have to go out and create it. You always have the virtual option: creating or joining discussion groups online. You can also search out like-minded people by taking classes on related subjects or joining a spiritual group that fits for you. You may even find a group of coworkers who are looking for something to do at lunch. If you keep your mind open and stay creative, you will be surprised who might find their way into your sangha. Visit www.mindfulnessforchocolatelovers.com to find new friends who also enjoy chocolate meditation.

EXERCISE: WHO'S IN YOUR SANGHA?

Using the ideas above, identify who you want to add to your sangha and how to make the connection. Identify at least five people.

Person(s)	How to make the connection
1.	
2.	
3.	
4.	
5.	

JOYFULNESS AS A WAY OF LIFE

I know you have lots of good reasons for putting extraordinary happiness off—you are too busy, you or someone you love is too ill, you do not have enough money, you are not a spiritual-type person, you cannot focus when you meditate, you have too much going on in your life right now. There is always a good, reasonable excuse—until the day you finally decide to say "no" to the rat race, "no" to ordinary happiness, "no" to the way everyone else is doing things, and finally "yes" to extraordinary happiness, to joy. In the end, it is a simple decision. You decide to take another path. You can start today—the wind is perfect!

There is a famous exercise that time management speakers use to illustrate priorities and time. First, they have a volunteer fill a mason jar as full as possible with rocks. Once everyone agrees that the jar is full, the instructor has the volunteer fill the same jar with pebbles and then sand, both of which tumble down to fill the spaces between the rocks. Once everyone is again convinced that the jar is now full, the instructor has the volunteer add water. The parallels with how we choose to use our time are obvious. Your big priorities are the big rocks. If you fill your jar with lesser priorities first—represented by the water, sand, and pebbles—you will not have space for the bigger ones. Your jar will always be full. You decide exactly how you fill it. When you make extraordinary happiness your first priority, your life will be filled with great things.

DOWN TO THE LAST BITE

I want to leave you with one last little morsel to savor. Whenever you are in doubt, give life a knowing smile. Like the Mona Lisa, you've got a secret and the whole world can tell. You know that more is possible, that the extraordinary life is within your grasp. Each day you take a moment to notice the colors of the flowers on your way out the door, linger for a moment when you feel a cool breeze on your face, laugh when the going gets rough, or choose gratifying work over the easy way out, you are doing it—moving toward the life we spend our lives trying to find. You know how to create it now. All it took was a few bites of chocolate.

Notes: Academic Bits and Pieces

CHAPTER 1. CHOCOLATE MEDITATION:
A TASTE OF THE GOOD LIFE

1. Jon Kabat-Zinn, *Full Catastrophe Living: Using the Wisdom of Your Body and Mind to Face Stress, Pain, and Illness* (New York: Delta, 1990), 142; Bob Stahl and Elisha Goldstein, *A Mindfulness-Based Stress Reduction Workbook* (New York: New Harbinger, 2010), 18–19.

2. D. C. Lau, trans., *Lao Tzu: Tao Te Ching* (New York: Penguin, 1963), 8–51.

3. Sheung-Tak Cheng, Pui Ki Tsui, and Jon H. M. Lam, "Improving Mental Health in Health Care Practitioners: Randomized Controlled Trial of a Gratitude Intervention," *Journal of Consulting and Clinical Psychology* 83, no. 1 (February 2015): 177–86, doi:10.1037/a0037895.

4. Steven R. H. Beach and Mark A. Whisman, "Affective Disorders," *Journal of Marital and Family Therapy* 38, no. 1 (January 2012): 201–19.

CHAPTER 2. FROM CHOCOHOLISM
TO CHOCOLATE SNOBBERY: BECOMING A
SEEKER OF EXTRAORDINARY HAPPINESS

1. Martin Seligman, *Authentic Happiness* (New York: Free Press, 2002), 3–102.

2. Alan Carr, *Positive Psychology: The Science of Happiness and Human Strengths* (New York: Brunner Routledge Press, 2004), 1–47.

3. David G. Myers and Ed Diener, "The Scientific Pursuit of Happiness," *Perspectives on Psychological Science* 13, no. 2 (March 2018): 218–25.

4. Ed Diener, Weiting Ng, James Harter, and Raksha Arora, "Wealth and Happiness across the World: Material Prosperity Predicts Life Evaluation, Whereas Psychosocial Prosperity Predicts Positive Feeling," *Journal of Personality and Social Psychology* 99, no. 1 (July 2010): 52–61.

5. Jordi Quoidbach, Elizabeth W. Dunn, K. V. Petrides, and Moira Miko-lajczak, "Money Giveth, Money Taketh Away: The Dual Effect of Wealth on Happiness," *Psychological Science*, 21, no. 6 (May 2010): 759–63.

6. Jan Delhey, "From Materialist to Post-Materialist Happiness? National Affluence and Determinants of Life Satisfaction in Cross-National Perspective," *Social Indicators Research* 97, no.1 (May 2010): 65–84.

7. Julian House, Sanford E. DeVoe, and Chen-Bo Zhong, "Too Impatient to Smell the Roses: Exposure to Fast Food Impedes Happiness," *Social Psychological and Personality Science* 5, no. 5 (November 2013): 534–41.

8. Joseph W. Alba and Elanor F. Williams, "Pleasure Principles: A Review of Research on Hedonic Consumption," *Journal of Consumer Psychology* 23, no. 1 (January 2013): 2–18.

9. Hannah P. Klug and Günter W. Maier, "Linking Goal Progress and Subjective Well-Being: A Meta-Analysis," *Journal of Happiness Studies* 16, no. 1 (February 2015): 37–65.

10. David J. Disabato, Todd B. Kashdan, Jerome L. Short, and Aaron Jarden, "What Predicts Positive Life Events that Influence the Course of Depression? A Longitudinal Examination of Gratitude and Meaning in Life," *Cognitive Therapy and Research* 41, no. 3 (June 2017): 444–58.

11. Bruce Chapman and Cahit Guven, "Revisiting the Relationship be-tween Marriage and Wellbeing: Does Marriage Quality Matter?" *Journal of Happiness Studies* 17, no. 2 (April 2016): 533–51.

12. Michael A. Cohn, Barbara L. Fredrickson, Stephanie L. Brown, Joseph A. Mikels, and Anne M. Conway, "Happiness Unpacked: Positive Emotions Increase Life Satisfaction by Building Resilience," *Emotion* 9, no. 3 (2009): 361–68.

13. Matthieu Ricard, *Happiness: A Guide to Developing Life's Most Important Skill* (New York: Brown & Co., 2007), 17–32.

CHAPTER 3. CHOCOLATE IS A VEGETABLE: MAPPING THE TRUTHS YOU LIVE BY

1. Pema Chödrön, *When Things Fall Apart: Heart Advice for Difficult Times* (Boulder, CO: Shambhala, 1997), 12.

2. Martha Beck, *Finding Your Own North Star: Claiming the Life You Were Meant to Live* (New York: Three Rivers Press, 2001), 1–37.

3. Martin Seligman, *Authentic Happiness* (New York: Free Press, 2002), 88.

4. Tara Brach, *Radical Acceptance: Embracing Your Life with the Heart of the Buddha* (New York: Bantam, 2004), 84.

5. Dalai Lama, *The Good Heart* (Boston: Wisdom Publications, 1996), 67–70.

6. Tosha Silver, *Outrageous Openness: Letting the Divine Take the Lead* (Alameda, CA: Urban Kali, 2011), 1–16.

CHAPTER 4. WHO MOVED MY CHOCOLATE: BEFRIENDING PROBLEMS, BEFRIENDING LIFE

1. Thich N. Hanh, *The Heart of Buddha's Teaching: Transforming Suffering into Peace, Joy & Liberation* (Berkeley, CA: Parallax, 1998), 9–12.

2. Ibid.

3. Benjamin M. Galvin, Amy E. Randel, Brian J. Collins, and Russell E. Johnson, "Changing the Focus of Locus (of Control): A Targeted Review of the Locus of Control Literature and Agenda for Future Research," *Journal of Organizational Behavior* 39, no. 7 (September 2018): 820–33, doi:10.1002/job.2275.

4. Viktor Frankl, *Man's Search for Meaning* (Boston: Beacon, 1963), 15–101.

5. Pema Chödrön, *When Things Fall Apart: Heart Advice for Difficult Times* (Boulder, CO: Shambhala, 1997), 12.

6. Jack Kornfield, *A Path with Heart: A Guide Through the Perils and Promises of Spiritual Life* (New York: Bantam, 1993), 80.

7. Richard C. Schwartz, *Internal Family Systems Therapy* (New York: Guilford, 1995), 27–60.

CHAPTER 5. ONE BITE IS ALL IT TAKES: MINDFULLY WAKING UP TO YOUR LIFE

1. Jon Kabat-Zinn, *Full Catastrophe Living: Using the Wisdom of Your Body and Mind to Face Stress, Pain, and Illness* (New York: Delta, 1990), 31–40.

2. Diane Gehart, *Mindfulness and Acceptance in Couple and Family Therapy* (New York: Springer, 2012), 112.

3. Mihaly Csikszentmihalyi, *Flow: The Psychology of Optimal Experience* (New York: Harper, 2008), 39–40.

4. Ruth A. Baer, "Mindfulness Training as a Clinical Intervention: A Conceptual and Empirical Review," *Clinical Psychology: Science and Practice* 10, no. 2 (June 2003): 125–43, doi:10.1093/clipsy/bpg015; A. Chiesa and A. Serretti, "A Systematic Review of Neurobiological and Clinical Features of Mindfulness Meditations," *Psychological Medicine: A Journal of Research in Psychiatry and the Allied Sciences* 40, no. 8 (August 2010): 1239–52, doi:10.1017/S0033291709991747;

Fabrizio Didonna, ed., *Clinical Handbook of Mindfulness* (New York: Springer Science + Business Media, 2009), doi:10.1007/978-0-387-09593-6.

5. Rick Hanson, *The Buddha's Brain: The Practical Neuroscience of Happiness, Love, and Wisdom* (Oakland, CA: New Harbinger, 2009), 24–48; Daniel Goleman and Richard J. Davidson, *Altered Traits: Science Reveals How Meditation Changes Your Mind, Brain, and Body* (New York: Avery, 2017), 192–99.

6. Daniel J. Siegel, *Mindsight* (New York: Norton, 2007), 15.

7. Daniel J. Siegel, *The Mindful Brain* (New York: Norton, 2007), xxvi.

8. Richard J. Davidson, Jon Kabat-Zinn, Jessica Schumacher, Melissa Rosenkranz, Daniel Muller, Saki F. Santorelli, et al., "Alterations in Brain and Immune Function Produced by Mindfulness Meditation," *Psychosomatic Medicine* 65 (July 2003): 564–70.

9. Do-Hyung Kang, Hang Joon Jo, Wi Hoon Jung, Sun Hyung Kim, Ye-Ha Jung, Chi-Hoon Choi, Ul Soon Lee, Seung Chan An, Joon Hwan Jang, and Jun Soo Kwon, "The Effect of Meditation on Brain Structure: Cortical Thickness Mapping and Diffusion Tensor Imaging," *Social Cognitive and Affective Neuroscience* 8, no. 1 (January 2013): 27–33, doi:10.1093/scan/nss056.

10. Paul A. M. van den Hurk, Fabio Giommi, Stan C. Gielen, Anne E. M. Speckens, and Henk P. Barendregt, "Greater Efficiency in Attentional Processing Related to Mindfulness Meditation," *Quarterly Journal of Experimental Psychology* 63, no. 6 (June 2010): 1168–80, doi:10.1080/17470210903249365.

11. Britta K. Hölzel, James Carmody, Mark Vangel, Christina Congleton, Sita M. Yerramsetti, Tim Gard, and Sara W. Lazar. "Mindfulness Practice Leads to Increases in Regional Brain Gray Matter Density." *Psychiatry Research: Neuroimaging* 191, no. 1 (January 30, 2011): 36–43, doi:10.1016/j.pscychresns.2010.08.006.

12. Britta K. Hölzel, James Carmody, Karleyton C. Evans, Elizabeth A. Hoge, Jeffery A. Dusek, Lucas Morgan, Roger K. Pitman, and Sara W. Lazar, "Stress Reduction Correlates with Structural Changes in the Amygdala," *Social Cognitive and Affective Neuroscience* 5, no. 1 (March 2010): 11–17, doi:10.1093/scan/nsp034.

13. Peter Vestergaard-Poulsen, Martijn van Beek, Joshua Skewes, Carsten R. Bjarkam, Michael Stubberup, Jes Bertelsen, and Andreas Roepstorff, "Long-Term Meditation Is Associated with Increased Gray Matter Density in the Brain Stem," *NeuroReport: For Rapid Communication of Neuroscience Research* 20, no. 2 (January 2009): 170–74, doi:10.1097/WNR.0b013e328320012a.

14. Thich N. Hanh, *Peace Is Every Step: The Path of Mindfulness in Everyday Life* (New York: Bantam, 1992), 26.

15. Dhruv Zocchi, Gunther Wennemuth, and Yuki Oka, "The Cellular Mechanism for Water Detection in the Mammalian Taste System," *Nature Neuroscience* 20, no. 7 (May 2017): 927–33, doi:10.1038/nn.4575.

CHAPTER 6. WITH OR WITHOUT NUTS:
CRAZY WISDOM AND THE BACK DOOR TO HAPPINESS

1. P. S. Fry, "Perfectionism, Humor, and Optimism as Moderators of Health Outcomes and Determinants of Coping Styles of Women Executives," *Genetic, Social, and General Psychology Monographs* 121, no. 2 (May 1995): 211–45.

2. Jessica Mesmer-Magnus, David J. Glew, and Chockalingam Viswesvaran, "A Meta-Analysis of Positive Humor in the Workplace," *Journal of Managerial Psychology* 27, no. 2 (February 2012): 155–90.

3. L. Saxon, N. Makhashvili, I. Chikovani, M. Seguin, M. McKee, V. Patel, J. Bisson, and B. Roberts, "Coping Strategies and Mental Health Outcomes of Conflict-Affected Persons in the Republic of Georgia," *Epidemiology and Psychiatric Sciences* 26, no. 3 (June 2017): 276–86.

4. Heiki A. Winterheld, Jeffrey A. Simpson, and Minda M. Oriña, "It's In the Way That You Use It: Attachment and the Dyadic Nature of Humor During Conflict Negotiation in Romantic Couples," *Personality and Social Psychology Bulletin* 39, no. 4 (April 2013): 496–508.

5. Rod A. Martin, Patricia Puhlik-Doris, Gwen Larsen, Jeanette Gray, and Kelly Weir, "Individual Differences in Uses of Humor and Their Relation to Psychological Well-Being: Development of the Humor Styles Questionnaire," *Journal of Research in Personality* 37, no. 1 (February 2003): 48–75.

6. Nadia Maiolino and Nick Kuiper, "Examining the Impact of a Brief Humor Exercise on Psychological Well-Being," *Translational Issues in Psychological Science* 2, no. 1 (2016), 4–13.

7. Nicholas Kuiper, Gillian Kirsh, and Nadia Maiolino, "Identity and Intimacy Development, Humor Styles, and Psychological Well-Being," *Identity: An International Journal of Theory and Research* 16, no. 2 (April 2016): 115–25.

8. Wes Nisker, *The Essential Crazy Wisdom* (Emeryville, CA: 10 Speed Press, 2001), 11–30; Chogyam Trungpa, *Crazy Wisdom* (Boulder, CO: Shambhala, 2001), 21.

9. Heinrich Dumoulin, *Zen Enlightenment: Origins and Meaning* (New York: Weatherhill, 1989), 65.

10. Peter Harvey, *An Introduction to Buddhism* (Cambridge, UK: Cambridge University Press, 1995), 273–75.

11. Jetson Milarepa, *Drinking the Mountain Stream: Songs of Tibet's Beloved Saint, Milarepa*, trans. Trunga Rinpoche and Brian Cutillo (Boston: Wisdom Publications, 1995), 5–9.

12. Ibid., 62, 63, 73–80, 81, 144.

13. Bradford Keeney, *Everyday Soul* (New York: Riverhead Press, 1997), 48.

14. Ibid., 57.

15. Steven Heine, *Opening a Mountain: Koans of the Zen Masters* (Cary: Oxford University Press, 2002), 4.

16. Keeney, *Everyday Soul*, 65–68.

CHAPTER 7. FIERCE COMPASSION: OPENING YOUR HEART TO MILK, WHITE, AND DARK

1. Tara Brach, *Radical Acceptance: Embracing Your Life with the Heart of the Buddha* (New York: Bantam, 2004), 198–245.

2. Sharon Salzburg, *Loving Kindness: The Revolutionary Art of Happiness* (Boston: Shambhala, 1995), 33–47.

3. Edo Shonin, William Gordon, Angelo Compare, Masood Zangeneh, and Mark Griffiths, "Buddhist-Derived Loving-Kindness and Compassion Meditation for the Treatment of Psychopathology: A Systematic Review," *Mindfulness* 6, no. 5 (2015): 1161–80.

4. Christina Luberto, M. Shinday, Nina Song, Rhayun Philpotts, Lisa Park, L. Fricchione, and Elyse Yeh, "A Systematic Review and Meta-Analysis of the Effects of Meditation on Empathy, Compassion, and Prosocial Behaviors," *Mindfulness* 9, no. 3 (2018): 708–24.

5. Monica Leppma and Mark E. Young, "Loving-Kindness Meditation and Empathy: A Wellness Group Intervention for Counseling Students," *Journal of Counseling & Development* 94, no. 3 (July 2016): 297–305.

6. David T. Weibel, Andrew S. McClintock, and Timothy Anderson, "Does Loving-Kindness Meditation Reduce Anxiety? Results from a Randomized Controlled Trial," *Mindfulness* 8, no. 3 (2017): 565–71.

7. Helen Y. Weng, Breanna Schuyler, and Richard J. Davidson, "The Impact of Compassion Meditation Training on the Brain and Prosocial Behavior," in *The Oxford Handbook of Compassion Science*, ed. Emma M. Seppälä et al., 133–46 (New York: Oxford University Press, 2017).

8. Michail Mantzios and Janet C. Wilson, "Exploring Mindfulness and Mindfulness with Self-Compassion-Centered Interventions to Assist Weight Loss: Theoretical Considerations and Preliminary Results of a Randomized Pilot Study," *Mindfulness* 6, no. 4 (2015): 824–35.

9. Elizabeth A. Hoge, Maxine Chen, Esther Orr, Christina Metcalf, Laura Fischer, Mark Pollack, Immaculata Devivo, and Naomi Simon, "Loving-Kindness Meditation Practice Associated with Longer Telomeres in Women," *Brain, Behavior, and Immunity* 32 (August 2013): 159–63.

10. Barbara Fredrickson, Aaron Boulton, Ann Firestine, Patty Van Cappellen, Sara Algoe, Mary Brantley, Sumi Kim, Jeffrey Brantley, and Sharon Salzberg, "Positive Emotion Correlates of Meditation Practice: A Comparison of

Mindfulness Meditation and Loving-Kindness Meditation," *Mindfulness* 8, no. 6 (2017): 1623–33.

11. Thorsten Barnhofer, Tobias Chittka, Helen Nightingale, Claire Visser, and Catherine Crane, "State Effects of Two Forms of Meditation on Prefrontal EEG Asymmetry in Previously Depressed Individuals," *Mindfulness* 1, no. 1 (2010): 21–27.

12. Tatia Lee, Mei-Kei Leung, Wai-Kai Hou, Joey C. Y. Tang, Jing Yin, Kwok-Fai So, Chack-Fan Chan, and Chetwyn C. H. Ben Hamed, "Distinct Neural Activity Associated with Focused-Attention Meditation and Loving-Kindness Meditation," *Plos ONE* 7, no. 8 (August 2012): 4e40054, doi: 10.1371/journal.pone.0040054.

13. Martin Buber, *I and Thou*, trans. Walter Kaufman (Edinburgh: T & T Clark, 1958), 51–53.

14. Brach, *Radical Acceptance*, 243–45.

CHAPTER 8. THERE'S NO WRONG WAY TO EAT A REESE'S—OR IS THERE? ETHICS AND HAPPINESS

1. Christopher Peterson and Martin Seligman, *Character Strengths and Virtues* (Oxford: Oxford University Press, 2004), 3–52.

2. Ibid.

3. Ibid.

4. Robert A. Emmons and Robin Stern, "Gratitude as a Psychotherapeutic Intervention," *Journal of Clinical Psychology* 69, no. 8 (August 2013): 846–55.

5. Marta Jackowska, Jennie Brown, Amy Ronaldson, and Andrew Steptoe, "The Impact of a Brief Gratitude Intervention on Subjective Well-Being, Biology and Sleep," *Journal of Health Psychology* 21, no. 10 (October 2016): 2207–17.

6. Martin Seligman, Tracy A. Steen, Nansook Park, and Christopher Peterson, "Positive Psychology Progress: Empirical Validation of Interventions," *American Psychologist* 60, no. 5 (July August 2005): 410 21.

7. Y. Joel Wong, Jesse Owen, Nicole T. Gabana, Joshua W. Brown, Sydney Mcinnis, Paul Toth, and Lynn Gilman, "Does Gratitude Writing Improve the Mental Health of Psychotherapy Clients? Evidence from a Randomized Controlled Trial," *Psychotherapy Research* 28, no. 2 (March 2018): 192–202.

8. Thich Nhat Hanh, *The Heart of Buddha's Teaching: Transforming Suffering Into Peace, Joy & Liberation* (Berkeley, CA: Parallax, 1998), 55.

9. Daniel Ladinsky, *Love Poems from God* (London: Penguin, 2002), 188.

10. Sadaf Akhtar and Jane Barlow, "Forgiveness Therapy for the Promotion of Mental Well-Being: A Systematic Review and Meta-Analysis," *Trauma, Violence, & Abuse* 19, no. 1 (January 2018): 107–22.

11. Lenka Tenklova and Alena Slezackova, "Differences between Self-Forgiveness and Interpersonal Forgiveness in Relation to Mental Health," *Journal of the Indian Academy of Applied Psychology* 42, no. 2 (July 2016): 282–90.

12. Loren L. Toussaint, Grant S. Shields, and George M. Slavich, "Forgiveness, Stress, and Health: A 5-Week Dynamic Parallel Process Study," *Annals of Behavioral Medicine* 50, no. 5 (October 2016): 727–35.

13. Martin Seligman, *Authentic Happiness* (New York: Free Press, 2002), 176; Mihaly Csikszentmihalyi and I. S. Csikszentmihalyi, *Optimal Experience: Psychological Studies of Flow in Consciousness* (Cambridge, UK: Cambridge University Press, 1992), 71–93.

14. Seligman, *Authentic Happiness*, 51–55.

CHAPTER 9. ARTIFICIAL CHOCOLATE AND COMFORT FOODS: DANGERS AND PITFALLS ON THE PATH

1. Christine Carter, *Raising Happiness: 10 Simple Steps for More Joyful Kids and Happier Parents* (New York: Ballantine, 2010), 48–53.

2. Ibid.

3. Martin Seligman, *Authentic Happiness* (New York: Free Press, 2002), 48.

4. Chogyam Trungpa, *Crazy Wisdom* (Boulder, CO: Shambhala, 2001), 3–13.

5. Christiane Northrup, *Dodging Energy Vampires: An Empath's Guide to Evading Relationships that Drain You and Restoring Your Health and Power* (New York: Hay House, 2018), 27–42.

6. Marsha M. Linehan, *Cognitive-Behavioral Treatment of Borderline Personality Disorder* (New York: Guilford, 1993), 97–119.

7. Martha Stout, *The Sociopath Next Door* (New York: Penguin, 2006), 107–9.

CHAPTER 10. THE ART OF SAVORING: JOYFULNESS AS A WAY OF LIFE

1. Coleman Barks, trans., *Rumi: The Book of Love* (San Francisco: Harper Books, 2003), 27–29.

2. Bill O'Hanlon, *Do One Thing Different* (New York: William Morrow, 2000), 1–25.

Bibliography

Akhtar, Sadaf, and Jane Barlow. "Forgiveness Therapy for the Promotion of Mental Well-Being: A Systematic Review and Meta-Analysis." *Trauma, Violence, & Abuse* 19, no. 1 (January 2018): 107–22.

Alba, Joseph W., and Elanor F. Williams. "Pleasure Principles: A Review of Research on Hedonic Consumption." *Journal of Consumer Psychology* 23, no. 1 (January 2013): 2–18.

Baer, Ruth A. "Mindfulness Training as a Clinical Intervention: A Conceptual and Empirical Review." *Clinical Psychology: Science and Practice* 10, no. 2 (June 2003): 125–43. doi:10.1093/clipsy/bpg015.

Barks, Coleman, trans. *Rumi: The Book of Love.* San Francisco: Harper Books, 2003.

Barnhofer, Thorsten, Tobias Chittka, Helen Nightingale, Claire Visser, and Catherine Crane. "State Effects of Two Forms of Meditation on Prefrontal EEG Asymmetry in Previously Depressed Individuals." *Mindfulness* 1, no. 1 (2010): 21–27.

Beach, Steven R. H., and Mark A. Whisman. "Affective Disorders." *Journal of Marital and Family Therapy* 38, no. 1 (January 2012): 201–19.

Beck, Martha. *Finding Your Own North Star: Claiming the Life You Were Meant to Live.* New York: Three Rivers Press, 2001.

Brach, Tara. *Radical Acceptance: Embracing Your Life with the Heart of the Buddha.* New York: Bantam, 2004.

Buber, Martin. *I and Thou.* Translated by Walter Kaufman. Edinburgh: T & T Clark, 1958.

Carr, Alan. *Positive Psychology: The Science of Happiness and Human Strengths.* New York: Brunner Routledge Press, 2004.

Carter, Christine. *Raising Happiness: 10 Simple Steps for More Joyful Kids and Happier Parents.* New York: Ballantine, 2010.

Chapman, Bruce, and Cahit Guven. "Revisiting the Relationship between Marriage and Wellbeing: Does Marriage Quality Matter?" *Journal of Happiness Studies* 17, no. 2 (April 2016): 533–51.

Cheng, Sheung-Tak, Pui Ki Tsui, and Jon H. M. Lam. "Improving Mental Health in Health Care Practitioners: Randomized Controlled Trial of a Gratitude Intervention." *Journal of Consulting and Clinical Psychology* 83, no.1 (February 2015): 177–86. doi:10.1037/a0037895.

Chiesa, A., and A. Serretti. "A systematic review of neurobiological and clinical features of mindfulness meditations." *Psychological Medicine: A Journal of Research in Psychiatry and the Allied Sciences* 40, no. 8 (August 2010): 1239–52. doi:10.1017/S0033291709991747

Chödrön, Pema. *When Things Fall Apart: Heart Advice for Difficult Times*. Boulder, CO: Shambhala, 1997.

Cohn, Michael A., Barbara L. Fredrickson, Stephanie L. Brown, Joseph A. Mikels, and Anne M. Conway. "Happiness Unpacked: Positive Emotions Increase Life Satisfaction by Building Resilience." *Emotion* 9, no. 3 (2009): 361–68.

Csikszentmihályi, Mihaly. *Flow: The Psychology of Optimal Experience*. New York: Harper, 2008.

Csikszentmihalyi, Mihaly, and I. S. Csikszentmihalyi. *Optimal Experience: Psychological Studies of Flow in Consciousness*. Cambridge, UK: Cambridge University Press, 1992.

Dalai Lama. *The Good Heart*. Boston: Wisdom Publications, 1996.

Davidson, Richard J., Jon Kabat-Zinn, Jessica Schumacher, Melissa Rosenkranz, Daniel Muller, Saki F. Santorelli, et al. "Alterations in Brain and Immune Function Produced by Mindfulness Meditation." *Psychosomatic Medicine* 65 (July 2003): 564–70.

Delhey, Jan. "From Materialist to Post-Materialist Happiness? National Affluence and Determinants of Life Satisfaction in Cross-National Perspective." *Social Indicators Research* 97, no.1 (May 2010): 65–84.

Didonna, Fabrizio, ed. *Clinical Handbook of Mindfulness*. New York: Springer Science + Business Media, 2009. doi:10.1007/978-0-387-09593-6.

Diener, Ed, Weiting Ng, James Harter, and Raksha Arora. "Wealth and Happiness across the World: Material Prosperity Predicts Life Evaluation, Whereas Psychosocial Prosperity Predicts Positive Feeling." *Journal of Personality and Social Psychology* 99, no. 1 (July 2010): 52–61.

Disabato, David J., Todd B. Kashdan, Jerome L. Short, and Aaron Jarden. "What Predicts Positive Life Events that Influence the Course of Depression? A Longitudinal Examination of Gratitude and Meaning in Life." *Cognitive Therapy and Research* 41, no. 3 (June 2017): 444–58.

Dumoulin, Heinrich. *Zen Enlightenment: Origins and Meaning*. New York: Weatherhill, 1989.

Emmons, Robert A., and Robin Stern. "Gratitude as a Psychotherapeutic Intervention." *Journal of Clinical Psychology* 69, no. 8 (August 2013): 846–55.

Frankl, Viktor. *Man's Search for Meaning*. Boston: Beacon, 1963.

Fredrickson, Barbara, Aaron Boulton, Ann Firestine, Patty Van Cappellen, Sara Algoe, Mary Brantley, Sumi Kim, Jeffrey Brantley, and Sharon Salzberg. "Positive Emotion Correlates of Meditation Practice: A Comparison of Mindfulness Meditation and Loving-Kindness Meditation." *Mindfulness* 8, no. 6 (2017): 1623–33.

Fry, P. S. "Perfectionism, Humor, and Optimism as Moderators of Health Outcomes and Determinants of Coping Styles of Women Executives." *Genetic, Social, and General Psychology Monographs* 121, no. 2 (May 1995): 211–45.

Galvin, Benjamin M., Amy E. Randel, Brian J. Collins, and Russell E. Johnson. "Changing the Focus of Locus (of Control): A Targeted Review of the Locus of Control Literature and Agenda for Future Research." *Journal of Organizational Behavior* 39, no. 7 (September 2018). doi:10.1002/job.2275.

Gehart, Diane. *Mindfulness and Acceptance in Couple and Family Therapy.* New York: Springer, 2012.

Goldeman, Daniel, and Richard J. Davidson. *Altered Traits: Science Reveals How Meditation Changes Your Mind, Brain, and Body.* New York: Avery, 2017.

Hanh, Thich N. *The Heart of Buddha's Teaching: Transforming Suffering into Peace, Joy & Liberation.* Berkeley, CA: Parallax, 1998.

———. *Peace Is Every Step: The Path of Mindfulness in Everyday Life.* New York: Bantam, 1992.

Hanson, Rick. *The Buddha's Brain: The Practical Neuroscience of Happiness, Love, and Wisdom.* Oakland, CA: New Harbinger, 2009.

Harvey, Peter. *An Introduction to Buddhism.* Cambridge, UK: Cambridge University Press, 1995.

Heine, Steven. *Opening a Mountain: Koans of the Zen Masters.* Cary: Oxford University Press, 2002.

Hoge, Elizabeth, Maxine Chen, Esther Orr, Christina Metcalf, Laura Fischer, Mark Pollack, Immaculata Devivo, and Naomi Simon. "Loving-kindness Meditation Practice Associated with Longer Telomeres in Women." *Brain, Behavior, and Immunity* 32 (August 2013): 159–63.

Hölzel, Britta K., James Carmody, Karleyton C. Evans, Elizabeth A. Hoge, Jeffery A. Dusek, Lucas Morgan, Roger K. Pitman, and Sara W. Lazar. "Stress Reduction Correlates with Structural Changes in the Amygdala." *Social Cognitive and Affective Neuroscience* 5, no. 1 (March 2010): 11–17. doi:10.1093/scan/nsp034.

Hölzel, Britta K., James Carmody, Mark Vangel, Christina Congleton, Sita M. Yerramsetti, Tim Gard, and Sara W. Lazar. "Mindfulness Practice Leads to Increases in Regional Brain Gray Matter Density." *Psychiatry Research: Neuroimaging* 191, no. 1 (January 30, 2011): 36–43. doi:10.1016/j.pscychresns.2010.08.006.

House, Julian, Sanford E. DeVoe, and Chen-Bo Zhong. "Too Impatient to Smell the Roses: Exposure to Fast Food Impedes Happiness." *Social Psychological and Personality Science* 5, no. 5 (November 2013): 534–41.

Jackowska, Marta, Jennie Brown, Amy Ronaldson, and Andrew Steptoe. "The Impact of a Brief Gratitude Intervention on Subjective Well-Being, Biology and Sleep." *Journal of Health Psychology* 21, no. 10 (October 2016): 2207–17.

Kabat-Zinn, Jon. *Full Catastrophe Living: Using the Wisdom of Your Body and Mind to Face Stress, Pain, and Illness.* New York: Delta, 1990.

Kang, Do-Hyung, Hang Joon Jo, Wi Hoon Jung, Sun Hyung Kim, Ye-Ha Jung, Chi-Hoon Choi, Ul Soon Lee, Seung Chan An, Joon Hwan Jang, and Jun Soo Kwon. "The Effect of Meditation on Brain Structure: Cortical Thickness Mapping and Diffusion Tensor Imaging." *Social Cognitive and Affective Neuroscience* 8, no. 1 (January 2013): 27–33. doi:10.1093/scan/nss056.

Keeney, Bradford. *Everyday Soul.* New York: Riverhead Press, 1997.

Khyentese Rinpoche, Dilgo, and Padampa Sangye. *The Hundred Verses of Advice: Tibetan Buddhist Teachings on What Matters Most.* Translated by Padmakara Translation Group. Boston: Shambhala, 2006.

Klug, Hannah P., and Günter W. Maier. "Linking Goal Progress and Subjective Well-Being: A Meta-Analysis." *Journal of Happiness Studies* 16, no. 1 (February 2015): 37–65.

Kornfield, Jack. *A Path with Heart: A Guide Through the Perils and Promises of Spiritual Life.* New York: Bantam, 1993.

Kuiper, Nicholas, Gillian Kirsh, and Nadia Maiolino. "Identity and Intimacy Development, Humor Styles, and Psychological Well-Being." *Identity: An International Journal of Theory and Research* 16, no. 2 (April 2016): 115–25.

Ladinsky, Daniel. *Love Poems from God.* London: Penguin, 2002.

Lau, D. C. *Lao Tzu: Tao Te Ching.* New York: Penguin, 1963.

Lee, Tatia M. C., Mei-Kei Leung, Wai-Kai Hou, Joey C. Y. Tang, Jing Yin, Kwok-Fai So, Chack-Fan Chan, and Chetwyn C. H. Ben Hamed. "Distinct Neural Activity Associated with Focused-Attention Meditation and Loving-Kindness Meditation." *Plos ONE* 7, no. 8 (August 2012): 4e40054. doi:10.1371/journal.pone.0040054.

Leppma, Monica, and Mark E. Young. "Loving-Kindness Meditation and Empathy: A Wellness Group Intervention for Counseling Students." *Journal of Counseling & Development* 94, no. 3 (July 2016): 297–305.

Linehan, Marsha M. *Cognitive-Behavioral Treatment of Borderline Personality Disorder.* New York: Guilford, 1993.

Luberto, Christina, M. Shinday, Nina Song, Rhayun Philpotts, Lisa Park, L. Fricchione, and Elyse Yeh. "A Systematic Review and Meta-Analysis of the Effects of Meditation on Empathy, Compassion, and Prosocial Behaviors." *Mindfulness* 9, no. 3 (2018): 708–24.

Maiolino, Nadia, and Nick Kuiper. "Examining the Impact of a Brief Humor Exercise on Psychological Well-Being." *Translational Issues in Psychological Science* 2, no. 1 (2016), 4–13.

Mantzios, Michail, and Janet C. Wilson. "Exploring Mindfulness and Mindfulness with Self-Compassion-Centered Interventions to Assist Weight Loss:

Theoretical Considerations and Preliminary Results of a Randomized Pilot Study." *Mindfulness* 6, no. 4 (2015): 824–35.

Martin, Rod, Patricia Puhlik-Doris, Gwen Larsen, Jeanette Gray, and Kelly Weir. "Individual Differences in Uses of Humor and Their Relation to Psychological Well-Being: Development of the Humor Styles Questionnaire." *Journal of Research in Personality* 37, no. 1 (February 2003): 48–75.

Mesmer-Magnus, Jessica, David J. Glew, and Chockalingam Viswesvaran. "A Meta-Analysis of Positive Humor in the Workplace." *Journal of Managerial Psychology* 27, no. 2 (February 2012): 155–90.

Milarepa, Jetson. *Drinking the Mountain Stream: Songs of Tibet's Beloved Saint, Milarepa.* Translated by Trunga Rinpoche and Brian Cutillo. Boston: Wisdom Publications, 1995.

Myers, David G., and Ed Diener. "The Scientific Pursuit of Happiness." *Perspectives on Psychological Science* 13, no. 2 (March 2018): 218–25.

Nisker, Wes. *The Essential Crazy Wisdom.* Emeryville, CA: 10 Speed Press, 2001.

Northrup, Christiane. *Dodging Energy Vampires: An Empath's Guide to Evading Relationships that Drain You and Restoring Your Health and Power.* New York: Hay House, 2018.

O'Hanlon, Bill. *Do One Thing Different.* New York: William Morrow, 2000.

Peterson, Christopher, and Martin Seligman. *Character Strengths and Virtues.* Oxford: Oxford University Press, 2004.

Quoidbach, Jordi, Elizabeth W. Dunn, K. V. Petrides, and Moira Mikolajczak. "Money Giveth, Money Taketh Away: The Dual Effect of Wealth on Happiness." *Psychological Science* 21, no. 6 (May 2010): 759–63.

Ricard, Matthieu. *Happiness: A Guide to Developing Life's Most Important Skill.* New York: Brown & Co., 2007.

Salzburg, Sharon. *Loving Kindness: The Revolutionary Art of Happiness.* Boston: Shambhala, 1995.

Saxon, L., N. Makhashvili, I. Chikovani, M. Seguin, M. McKee, V. Patel, J. Bisson, and B. Roberts, "Coping Strategies and Mental Health Outcomes of Conflict-Affected Persons in the Republic of Georgia." *Epidemiology and Psychiatric Sciences* 26, no. 3 (June 2017): 276–86.

Schwartz, Richard C. *Internal Family Systems Therapy.* New York: Guilford, 1995.

Seligman, Martin. *Authentic Happiness.* New York: Free Press, 2002.

Seligman, Martin E., Tracy A. Steen, Nansook Park, and Christopher Peterson. "Positive Psychology Progress: Empirical Validation of Interventions." *American Psychologist* 60, no. 5 (July–August 2005): 410–21.

Shonin, Edo, William Gordon, Angelo Compare, Masood Zangeneh, and Mark Griffiths. "Buddhist-Derived Loving-Kindness and Compassion Meditation for the Treatment of Psychopathology: A Systematic Review." *Mindfulness* 6, no. 5 (2015): 1161–80.

Siegel, Daniel J. *The Mindful Brain.* New York: Norton, 2007.
————. *Mindsight.* New York: Norton, 2007.
Silver, Tosha. *Outrageous Openness: Letting the Divine Take the Lead.* Alameda, CA: Urban Kali, 2011.
Stahl, Bob, and Elisha Goldstein. *A Mindfulness-Based Stress Reduction Workbook.* New York: New Harbinger, 2010.
Stout, Martha. *The Sociopath Next Door.* New York: Penguin, 2006.
Tenklova, Lenka, and Alena Slezackova. "Differences between Self-Forgiveness and Interpersonal Forgiveness in Relation to Mental Health." *Journal of the Indian Academy of Applied Psychology* 42, no. 2 (July 2016): 282–90.
Toussaint, Loren L., Grant S. Shields, and George M. Slavich. "Forgiveness, Stress, and Health: A 5-Week Dynamic Parallel Process Study." *Annals of Behavioral Medicine* 50, no. 5 (October 2016): 727–35.
Trungpa, Chogyam. *Crazy Wisdom.* Boulder, CO: Shambhala, 2001.
van den Hurk, Paul A., Fabio Giommi, Stan C. Gielen, Anne E. M. Speckens, and Henk P. Barendregt. "Greater Efficiency in Attentional Processing Related to Mindfulness Meditation." *Quarterly Journal of Experimental Psychology* 63, no. 6 (June 2010): 1168–80. doi:10.1080/17470210903249365.
Vestergaard-Poulsen, Peter, Martijn van Beek, Joshua Skewes, Carsten R. Bjarkam, Michael Stubberup, Jes Bertelsen, and Andreas Roepstorff. "Long-Term Meditation Is Associated with Increased Gray Matter Density in the Brain Stem." *NeuroReport: For Rapid Communication of Neuroscience Research* 20, no. 2 (January 2009): 170–74. doi:10.1097/WNR.0b013e328320012a.
Weibel, David T., Andrew S. McClintock, and Timothy Anderson. "Does Loving-Kindness Meditation Reduce Anxiety? Results from a Randomized Controlled Trial." *Mindfulness* 8, no. 3 (2017): 565–71.
Weng, Helen Y., Breanna Schuyler, and Richard J. Davidson. "The Impact of Compassion Meditation Training on the Brain and Prosocial Behavior." In *The Oxford Handbook of Compassion Science,* edited by Emma M. Seppälä et al., 133–46. New York: Oxford University Press, 2017.
Winterheld, Heiki A., Jeffrey A. Simpson, and Minda M. Oriña. "It's In the Way That You Use It: Attachment and the Dyadic Nature of Humor during Conflict Negotiation in Romantic Couples." *Personality and Social Psychology Bulletin* 39, no. 4 (April 2013): 496–508.
Wong, Y. Joel, Jesse Owen, Nicole T. Gabana, Joshua W. Brown, Sydney Mcinnis, Paul Toth, and Lynn Gilman. "Does Gratitude Writing Improve the Mental Health of Psychotherapy Clients? Evidence from a Randomized Controlled Trial." *Psychotherapy Research* 28, no. 2 (March 2018): 192–202.
Zocchi, Dhruv, Gunther Wennemuth, and Yuki Oka. "The Cellular Mechanism for Water Detection in the Mammalian Taste System." *Nature Neuroscience* 20, no. 7 (May 2017): 927–33. doi:10.1038/nn.4575.

Acknowledgments

$\mathcal{T}$his book has evolved over many years, and so I cannot possibly thank everyone for their various contributions. However, I am particularly grateful to the following:

- *Bill O'Hanlon:* My writing mentor who encouraged and guided me from the beginning to end.
- *Clare Sobel:* Whose brilliant editing significantly improved the clarity of my writing and thought.
- *Diana Losey:* Who supported me in friendship and editing over the years of this book's evolution.
- *Stephanie Hanson:* My multitalented assistant who solved technical problems as well as provided feedback on the work.
- *Katie Asner Luckerman:* Who made the book trailer happen.
- *Guenther* and *Anna Gehart:* Who provided design assistance for the early drafts.
- *Carrie Wiita:* Who brought her creative talents to the website.
- *Bryna Weiss and Michael Luckerman:* Who generously shared their acting talents in the book trailer.
- *Brooklyn Hudson:* Who brought movie magic to the trailer.
- *Suzanne Staszak-Silva:* For her generous and resourceful editorial leadership.
- *Katie O'Brian:* For reaching out.
- *My boys, Michael and Alex:* Who patiently supported their mother while she wrote this book. They were, of course, rewarded with chocolate and meditation.

Index

absolute charm, 158
abuse, 60; sexual, 129, 142
accepting "what is," with
    compassion, 72
action, 3, 23; words versus, 159
affiliative humor, 99
Africa, 12, 107
aggressive humor, 100
aging, 118
agrarian societies, 16
Alba, Joseph W., 18
alcohol, 80
American chocolate, 11
Americas, 107
amygdala, 83
anger, 20
antidepressants, 83
antisocial personality disorder
    (sociopathy), 156
anxiety, 1
any-sense-will-do meditation, 92
apps, for mindfulness, 95
Arriba, 12
artificial chocolate, 149–51
arts, 107
atheism, 75
attachment reduction (Fourth Noble
    Truth), 49

attachments (Second Noble Truth),
    48, 49–50; external versus internal
    locus of control and, 50–52. See
    also non-attachment
attention. See mindfulness
Australia, 107
Australian National University, 19
Authentic Happiness (Seligman), 15
avoidance, 53
awareness: Mindfulness Awareness
    Practices, 95; quality of, 75; self-
    regulated, 72

beauty, unexpected, 6
Beck, Martha, 31
Befriending Meditation, 69–70
befriending problems, 57–58;
    advanced course in, 65;
    grief and, 65–69; identifying
    friendship potentials (step 4),
    61–62; identifying negative and
    positive effects of (step 2), 60–61;
    identifying problem (step 1),
    59–60; identifying reaction to
    (step 3), 61; identifying small steps
    (step 5), 62–63; worksheet for
    (exercise), 63–65
behavioral medicine, 77

Bielefeld University, 19
biofeedback, 74
black widows, 104–5
bodily sensations, 86
body reaction, 4
body scan, 86
borderline personality disorder, 155
boss, as snake, 162
boundaries, poor, 160
brain: built-in model of, 79;
    happiness and, 136–39;
    mindfulness effects on, 83
brain stem, wrist representing, 79
breath, 72; finding time for
    (exercise), 93; relation response
    and, 82; yoga and, 90–91
breath meditation, 88–89
British chocolate, 11
Buber, Martin, 125
Buddha, 31, 45, 48, 75
Buddhism. *See specific topics*
Buddhist psychology, 8
built-in model of brain, 79

California Institute of Technology,
    92
callousness, 160
Calm (mindfulness app), 95
Cameroon, 12
Carr, Alan, 15
Catherine of Sienna (Saint), 141
centering prayer, 77
Chapman, Bruce, 19
chewing, 4
children, 161–62, 170
chocolate meditation, 2–3; no. 1,
    3–4; no. 2, 54–55; no. 3, 147
Chödrön, Pema, 31, 57
choice, 58
Christian Centering Prayer, 95
Christianity, 107; compassion and,
    114; contemplative prayer and,

77, 85; cosmic maps and, 31;
    Judeo-Christian tradition, 49, 76;
    mandalas and, 45; pleasure and, 36
cognitive psychology, 50
Cohn, Michael, 20
colors, 3
comfort foods, 151–52
communication, 1
compassion, 113–14; accepting
    "what is" with, 72; Buddhist
    view of, 114; four relationship
    types and, 121–22; loving-
    kindness meditation and, 114–16;
    mindfulness and, 118–19; science
    of, 117–18. *See also* fierce
    compassion
concentration camps, 143
contemplative prayer, 77, 85
control: locus of control, 50–52;
    losing, 42–45; by snakes, 160
conventional wisdom, crazy wisdom
    compared to, *101*
cosmic maps, 26–29; destination
    for, 35; exercise for, *32–33*;
    "how" and, 36–38; joyriding
    and, 35–36; losing control and,
    42–45; mandalas and, 45–46;
    not knowing and, 42, 44–45;
    permanence versus impermanence
    and, 40–41; personal connections
    and, 39; pessimistic to enlightened
    responses, 41; road maps, divine
    as instructor and, 30–33; saying
    "yes" and, 43; surprise with, 44;
    surrender and, 33–35
three attitudes for, *41*; treasure maps,
    universe as gift giver and, 30;
    treasure maps versus road maps,
    29; treasure map versus road map
    quiz (exercise), *34–35*; updating,
    39–40
courage, 135

coworkers, as snake, 162
crazy-making, 160
crazy wisdom, 98: Bingo, *102*;
  Buddhist, 101; conventional
  wisdom compared to, *101*;
  discipline of, 109–10; first-aid kit
  or medicine bag, 111–12; "if you
  meet the Buddha on the road, kill
  him," 108–9; koans and, 103–4;
  Milarepa and, 106–8; science
  of humor and, 98–99; wrathful
  deities and, 104–6
criticism, 48, 111; deflecting, 160
Csikszentmihalyi, Mihaly, 74, 143, 144
curiosity, 61

Dalai Lama, 116, 120, 170
dance, 107
Daoism, 5
Davidson, Richard, 83
Day-in-the-Life Meditation, 123–24
dead poets, 170–71
deities, wrathful, 104–6
Delhey, Jan, 16
denial, of pleasure, 36
depression, 1, 50
destination, for cosmic maps, 35
Diener, Ed, 16
digital devices, 1
discipline: of crazy wisdom, 109–10;
  joyful, 163
discomfort, 53, 152–53
dishwashing meditation, 89–90
distraction, pleasure as, 36
divine, as instructor, 30–33
Dodging Energy Vampires (Northrup),
  154–55
Do One Thing Different (O'Hanlon),
  167–68
drama, 159
dream fulfillment, bringing happiness
  (myth no. 3), 18–19

easy, settling for what is, 149–51
Ecuador, 12
eggshells, walking on, 160–61
ego, 143; humility and, 139–41
Eightfold Path, 49
embracing life, 53–57
emotional outcome, of flow, 75
emotions: focusing on, 87; negative
  emotions reducing happiness,
  19–20; positive, 19–20
empathy, lack of, 160
enemies: learning fierce compassion
  from, 128–31; relationship with,
  121
energy vampires, 155. *See also* snakes
  (individuals with mental health
  disorders)
enlightened responses, pessimistic
  responses to (exercise), *41*
entitlement, 159–60
equanimity, 40, *41*
ethical life, 134
ethics, 49, 146–47
everyday life, mindfulness in, 89–92
Everyday Soul (Keeney), 107
exercises, 168–69; befriending
  problems worksheet, 63–65; for
  cosmic maps, *32–33*; examining
  map for happiness, *27–28*;
  exploring ordinary happiness,
  14–15; finding time to breathe,
  93; first steps to extraordinary
  happiness, 23; going with flow,
  146; gratitude journals, 137–38;
  I-Thou experiments, 126–27,
  128; locus of control quiz, *52*; for
  not knowing, *44–45*; paradise to
  joyriding, *38*; personal gratitude
  habit, 139; pessimistic responses to
  enlightened responses, *41*; raising
  the bar on happiness, 150–51;
  sangha and, 171; spreading

wisdom, 103–4; treasure map versus road map quiz, *34–35*
external locus of control, 50–52
external world, 22
extraordinary happiness, 22, 149; first steps to (exercise), 23; joy and, 166. *See also* cosmic maps

"faint" response, 79
faith, 56
falling in love, 119–21
family, 170
family members, as snake, 162
fear, wrathful deities and, 104–6
feeling, 4
fierce compassion, 116–17; happiness and, 132; learning from enemy, 128–31; learning from loved ones and friends, 127–28; learning from strangers, 122–27; learning from yourself, 131–32; love and, 119–21
fight-flight-freeze response, 53, 79, 83
Finding Your Own North Star (Beck), 31
first-aid kit, 111–12
First Noble Truth (suffering), 48, 49–50
fixed mind-set, 150
flow (flow state): going with (exercise), *146*; gratifications and, 143–44; mindfulness as not, 74–75
focus, 6, 84, 94; on emotions, 87; on journey, 37; refocusing, 82–83, 119; on thoughts, 87
following through, 1
Food Guide Pyramid, 25
forgiveness, 141–43
Four Noble Truths: attachment reduction (Fourth), 49; attachments (Second), 48, 49–52;

non-attachment (Third), 49, 53–70; suffering (First), 48, 49–50
Fourth Noble Truth (attachment reduction), 49
Francis (Saint), 170
Frankl, Viktor, 51–52
freedom, from forgiveness, 142–43
friends, 170; learning fierce compassion from, 127–28; relationship with, 121; as snake, 162
fully present, 84
future visions, 23

Gallup World Poll, 16
Gallup Organization, 16
gender, 20
gentleness, 84
George Mason University, 19
God, as gift giver, 30
gracious consumer, 12
gratifications, 134; flow and, 143–44; immediate, 18; instant, 36; pleasure and, 145
gratitude, happiness and, 136–39
gratitude journals, 7, 136; exercise, 137–38
gray matter, 83
grief, 65–69
growth mind-set, 150
grudges, 142
guided meditation. *See* chocolate meditation
guilty pleasure, 25
Guven, Cahit, 19

habit: meditation as, 92; personal gratitude habit (exercise), *139*
habituation, 17
handy model, 79
happiness: distinguishing from pleasure, 35–36; dream fulfillment

bringing (myth no. 3), 18–19;
    examining map for (exercise), 27–
    28; fierce compassion and, 132;
    gratitude and, 136–39; healthiness
    increasing (myth no. 5), 20–21;
    joyful discipline and, 163; as life
    skill, 21–23; long-term marital,
    99; microwaved versus slow-
    cooked, 144–45; money leading
    to greater (myth no. 1), 15–17;
    negative emotions reducing (myth
    no. 4), 19–20; new formula for,
    21–22; pleasure bringing greater
    (myth no. 2), 17–18; positive
    psychology as science of, 15–21;
    raising the bar on (exercise),
    150–51. *See also* extraordinary
    happiness; ordinary happiness
Happy Holiday Bingo, *102*
Headspace (mindfulness app), 95
healthiness, increasing happiness
    (myth no. 5), 20–21
heart, opening of, 109
hedonistic treadmill, 18
hippocampus, 81–82, 83
Hong Kong, 119
hopelessness, 51
House, Julian, 18
humanity, 135
humility, ego and, 139–41
humor, 101; affiliative, 99; aggressive,
    100; science of, 98–99; self-
    defeating, 100; self-enhancing,
    99–100
Humor Style Questionnaire, 99

identity, 139–40
"if you meet the Buddha on the
    road, kill him," 108–9
I-It relationship, 125
immediate gratification, 18
impatience, 18

impermanence, 39; permanence
    versus, 40–41
individualist cultures, 19
inflexible patterns, 157
inner compass, 31
Insight Timer (mindfulness app), 95
instant gratification, 36
integrity, 37
intention, of flow, 75
interbeing, 39, 140–41
Internal Family Systems therapy, 69
internal locus of control, 50–52
intimacy, 1
"It," 5
Italian chocolate, 11
I-Thou relationships, 125;
    experiments (exercise), 126–27,
    128

Japan, 107
Java, 12
Jesus Christ, 114
Jewish-based meditation, 95
Jewish faith, 77
Jews, 143
John of the Cross (Saint), 170
Joke-a-Day, 110
journaling, gratitude, 7, 136, 137–38
journey, focus on, 37
joy, 166; embracing, 167; as way of
    life, 167
joyful discipline, 163
joyfulness, as way of life, 171–72
joyriding: cosmic maps and, 35–36;
    motorcycle maintenance and,
    145–46; paradise to (exercise), *38*;
    Judeo-Christian tradition, 49, 76
justice, 135

Kabat-Zinn, Jon, 2, 77
Kabbala, 77
Keating, Thomas, 77

Keeney, Bradford, 107, 108, 111
kindness, 84, 120
King, Martin Luther, Jr., 170
Klug, Hannah, 19
knowledge, 134
knuckles, representing prefrontal
    cortex, 80
koans, 103–4
Kornfield, Jack, 58, 122

Laotzu, 5
life skill, happiness as, 21–23
limbic system, 136; representing
    thumb, 79–80
"little things," 13, 65
living poets, 170–71
locus of control: external versus
    internal, 50–52; quiz for
    (exercise), *52*
long-term marital happiness, 99
losing control, 42–43; exercise for,
    44–45
lottery, 16–17, 152
love, 135; fierce compassion and,
    119–21; tough, 116–17. *See also*
    romantic partners
loved ones: learning fierce
    compassion from, 127–28;
    relationship with, 121
loving-kindness meditation (*metta*),
    114–16
Luberto, Christina, 117
lying, pathological, 161

magnetic resonance imaging (MRI),
    119
Maier, Günter, 19
major depressive disorder, 9
mandalas: center of, 46; filling in, 46;
    format for, 45; sub-themes of, 46
mapmaker, trust in, 33–35
maps. *See* cosmic maps

marriage: happiness and, 19, 99;
    laughter and, 99
Massachusetts General Hospital, 118
materialism, 17; postmaterialism, 16;
    spiritual, 153–54
meaning, 37
medicine bag, 111–12
meditation: any-sense-will-do, 92;
    Befriending, 69–70; breath,
    88–89; Day-in-the-Life, 123–24,
    125; dishwashing, 89–90; Jewish-
    based, 95; loving-kindness (*metta*),
    114–16; walking, 85–86; water,
    91–92. *See also* mindfulness
mental concentration, 49
mental health: forgiveness and,
    142; mindfulness improving
    disorders of, 77–78. *See also* snakes
    (individuals with mental health
    disorders)
metta (loving-kindness meditation),
    114–16
Mexican chocolate, 11, 12
microwaved happiness, 144–45
Milarepa, 106–8
"milk-white-or-dark" issue, 60
millennial couples, 1
mind: fixed mind-set, 150; growth
    mind-set, 150; on mindfulness,
    84; monkey, 72; opening of,
    109–10
mindfulness: apps, 95; breath
    meditation, 88–89; compassion
    and, 118–19; defined, 71–73;
    effects on brain, 83; in everyday
    life, 89–92; excuses for avoiding,
    92–94; flavors of, 85–87; mental
    health disorders improved by,
    77–78; mind on, 84; perfectionism
    and, 87–89; physical disorders
    improved by, 77; psychological
    benefits of, 78; reasons for, 76–79;

refocusing and, 82–83; relational
benefits of, 78; relation response
and breath and, 82; religion and,
75–76; resources for, 95; in society,
76; stress response and, 79–81;
training programs, 95; trauma and,
81–82; what it isn't, 73–75
Mindfulness Awareness Practices, 95
Mindfulness-Based Stress Reduction,
95
Mindfulness in Schools, 95
mindful waiting, 89
mind reaction, 4
mistakes, 142
money, leading to greater happiness
(myth no. 1), 15–17
monkey mind, 72
mood swings, 160–61
Mother Teresa, 125
motivation, 1
motorcycle maintenance, 145–46
MRI. *See* magnetic resonance
imaging
multitasking, 76
music, 107, 143
mystic traditions, 143–44
myths, 8; dream fulfillment bringing
happiness (myth no. 3), 18–19;
healthiness increasing happiness
(myth no. 5), 20–21; money
leading to greater happiness (myth
no. 1), 15–17; negative emotions
reducing happiness (myth no. 4),
19–20; pleasure bringing greater
happiness (myth no. 2), 17–18

narcissistic personality disorder,
155–56
negative effects, of problem,
identifying, 60–61
negative emotions, reducing
happiness (myth no. 4), 19–20

negative reinforcement, 2
neural integration, 81
neutral perspective, 31
New Age thinkers, 31
non-attachment (Third Noble
Truth), 49; befriending problems
and, 57–70; embracing life and,
53–57
nonjudgment, 84
nonjudgmental observation, 72
norms, social, 151
Northrup, Christiane, 154–55, 157
not knowing: exercise for, *44–45*;
wisdom of, 42

objective good health, 20
observation: nonjudgmental, 72; of
unwrapped chocolate, 3–4; of
wrapped chocolate, 3
O'Hanlon, Bill, 167–68
Ohio University, 117
optimism, 40, *41*
ordinary happiness, 13–15, 22;
comfort foods and, 151–52;
exploring (exercise), *14–15*
Outrageous Openness (Silver), 42
over-giving, 158

Papua New Guinea, 12
paradise to joyriding (exercise), *38*
pathological lying, 161
Peace Is Every Step (Thich Nhat
Hanh), 90
people pleasing, 51
perfectionism, 87–89
permanence, 39; impermanence
versus, 40–41
personal connections, cosmic maps
and, 39
personal gratitude habit (exercise),
139
personality shifts, 161

pervasive patterns, 157
pessimism, 40, *41*
pessimistic responses, to enlightened responses (exercise), *41*
Peterson, Christopher, 134, 138
physical disorders, mindfulness improving, 77
play, 57, 107, 108
pleasure, 6, 134, 143; bringing greater happiness (myth no. 2), 17–18; denial of, 36; distinguishing from happiness, 35–36; as distraction, 36; gratifications and, 145; guilty, 25
poets, dead and living, 170–71
poor boundaries, 160
positive effects, of problem, identifying, 60–61
positive emotions, 19–20
positive psychology, 8; dream fulfillment bringing happiness (myth no. 3), 18–19; ethical life and, 134; ethics and, 146–47; forgiveness and, 141–43; gratifications and flow and, 143–44; gratitude and happiness and, 136–39; healthiness increasing happiness (myth no. 5), 20–21; humility and ego and, 139–41; microwaved versus slow-cooked happiness and, 144–45; money leading to greater happiness (myth no. 1), 15–17; motorcycle maintenance and joyriding and, 145–46; negative emotions reducing happiness (myth no. 4), 19–20; pleasure bringing greater happiness (myth no. 2), 17–18; as science of happiness, 15–21; virtues and, 134–35; virtuous conduct and, 135–36
Positive Psychology (Carr), 15
positive reinforcement, 2

postindustrial societies, 16
postmaterialism, 16
prayer: centering, 77; Christian Centering Prayer, 95; contemplative, 77, 85
preference, 56–57, 60
prefrontal cortex, 81; knuckles representing, 80
preparation, problem as, 62
present moment, 5
problems: as preparation, 62; as teacher, 61–62. *See also* befriending problems
Psychology: Buddhist, 8; cognitive, 50. *See also* positive psychology
punishment, 160

quality of awareness, flow of, 75
Quoidbach, Dr., 16

racist comments, 100
reaction: body, 4; mind, 4; to problem, identifying, 61
reality, reshaping of, 7
receptiveness, 84
Reese's Peanut Butter Cup, 133
refocusing, 82–83, 119
regular practice, of mindfulness, 83
relational benefits, of mindfulness, 78
relation response, 82
relationships, 39; four types of, 121–22; I-It, 125; I-Thou, 125, 126–27, 128
relaxation technique, mindfulness as not, 73–74
religion: mindfulness and, 75–76. *See also* Christianity
religious groups, 170
Ricard, Matthieu, 21
road maps: divine as instructor and, 30–33; treasure maps versus, 29; treasure maps versus (quiz), 34–35

romantic partners: with children, 162; with no children, 161–62
Roosevelt, Eleanor, 116
Rumi, 166, 170
runner's high, 74

sadness, 20
samatha, 85
sangha, 39, 167; creating, 169–71; virtual, 171
Santo Domingo, 12
savoring, 165–66
saying "yes," 43
scent, 3, 4
science: of compassion, 117–18; of happiness, positive psychology as, 15–21; of humor, 98–99; Western, 77, 121
scientific research, on mindfulness, 71
Second Noble Truth (attachments), 48, 49–52
self, as snake, 162
self-defeating humor, 100
self-enhancing humor, 99–100
self-forgiveness, 142
self-regulated awareness, 72
self-worth, 51
Seligman, Martin, 15, 18, 134, 138, 144
settling, for what is easy, 149–51
sexist comments, 100
sexual abuse, 129, 142
Shamanic Christianity (Keeney), 107
shape, 3
Siegel, Dan, 79, 80
Silver, Tosha, 42
single-origin chocolates, 12
slow-cooked happiness, 144–45
slowing down, 6
small changes, 167
smirti (mindfulness), 71
snakes (individuals with mental health disorders): avoiding, 154–57; clear

signs of, 159–61; earliest warning signs of, 157–59; how to spot, 157; saving oneself from, 161–62
snobbery, 11–12
social norms, 151
society, mindfulness in, 76
The Sociopath Next Door (Stout), 156
sociopathy (antisocial personality disorder), 156
sorrow, embracing, 167
South American chocolate, 11
Spanish chocolate, 11
spiders, 104–5
spiritual development, 87
spiritual groups, 170
spirituality, 135, 138
spiritual materialism, 153–54
spiritual warrior, 132
splitting, 158
stopping thoughts, mindfulness as not, 74
story, 8
Stout, Martha, 156
Strangers: learning fierce compassion from, 122–27; relationship with, 121
stress response, 53, 79–80; "flipping your lid" and, 80–81
subjective good health, 20
suffering (First Noble Truth), 48, 49–50
surprise, 44
surrender, 33–35
Swiss chocolate, 11

Tankstelle, 113
Tanzania, 12
taste, 4
teacher, problem as, 61–62
TED Talks, 33
telomere length, 118
temperance, 135
texture, 4

Thich Nhat Hanh, 39, 90, 140
Third Noble Truth (non-
    attachment), 49, 53–70
thoughts: focusing on, 87; stopping,
    74
thumb, limbic system representing,
    79–80
Tibetan Book of the Dead, 104
Tibetans, 143
tonglen, 128–29
"too" perfect, snakes as, 158
torture, 143
tough love, 116–17
tragedy, 66
training programs, for mindfulness, 95
trance, mindfulness as not, 74
transcendence, 135, 138
trauma, 99; mindfulness and, 81–82
treasure maps; road maps versus, 29;
    road maps versus (quiz), 34–35;
    universe as gift giver and, 30
Trungpa, Chogyam, 153
trust, in mapmaker, 33–35

unexpected beauty, 6
universe, as gift giver, 30
University of Illinois, 16
University of London, 99
University of Massachusetts, 77
University of North Carolina, 99
University of Toronto, 18
University of Victoria, 98–99
University of Virginia, 12
University of Wisconsin, 83
updating, of cosmic maps, 39–40
U.S. Department of Agriculture, 25
utility, 32

vegetable, chocolate as, 25
victimization, 51

victim mentality, 158–59
vipassana, 85
virtual *sanghas*, 171
virtues, 134–35
virtuous conduct, 135–36, 144

waiting, mindful, 89
walking meditation, 85–86
walking on eggshells, 160–61
walnuts, 166
water, 91–92
water meditation, 91–92
wealth, 15–17
Weibel, David, 118
weight, 3
weight management, 118
Western psychologists, 50, 54
Western science, 77, 121
"what is," accepting with
    compassion, 72
"wide-angle lens" of wisdom, 40
Williams, Elanor F., 18
wisdom, 49, 134; of not knowing,
    42; spreading (exercise), 103–4;
    "wide-angle lens" of, 40. *See also*
    crazy wisdom
women, 20
words versus actions, 159
World Values Study, 16
worry, 57–58
wrathful deities, 104–6
wrist, representing brain stem, 79

"yes," saying, 43
yoga, 90–91
yourself: learning fierce compassion
    from, 131–32; relationship with,
    121

Zen Buddhism, 92, 103

About the Author

Diane R. Gehart, PhD, is a professor in the Marriage and Family Therapy Program at California State University, Northridge. She has authored numerous books, including *Mindfulness and Acceptance in Couple and Family Therapy*, *Mastering Competencies in Family Therapy*, and *Theory and Treatment Planning in Counseling and Psychotherapy*; she coedited *Collaborative Therapy: Relationships and Conversations that Make a Difference*. Her areas of research and specialty include mindfulness, Buddhist psychology, couple and family therapy, trauma, sexual abuse, gender, children, relationships, client advocacy, mental health recovery, and psychotherapy theories. She speaks internationally, having given workshops to professional and general audiences in the United States, Canada, Europe, and Mexico. Her research has been featured in newspapers, radio shows, and television worldwide. She maintains a private practice in Agoura Hills, California, specializing in couples, families, adolescents, trauma, life transitions, and difficult-to-treat cases. You can learn more about her at www.dianegehart.com, www.mindfulschool.net, www.masteringcompetencies.com, and her YouTube channel, www.youtube.com/c/DianeRGehartPhD.